MW00942677

Meth Monster

The story of a resurrected life

by

Timothy Blaine

Bloomington, IN Milton Keynes, UK

AuthorHouse™
1663 Liberty Drive, Suite 200
Bloomington, IN 47403
www.authorhouse.com
Phone: 1-800-839-8640

AuthorHouse™ UK Ltd.
500 Avebury Boulevard
Central Milton Keynes, MK9 2BE
www.authorhouse.co.uk
Phone: 08001974150

First published by AuthorHouse 11/14/2006

ISBN: 978-1-4259-7151-9 (sc)

Printed in the United States of America
Bloomington, Indiana

This book is printed on acid-free paper.

"Let everything that has breath praise the Lord"

Dedication

This book is dedicated to the loving memory of Jimmy Baruch, Roosevelt Jackson, and Henry "Enrique" Trujillo, Jr.

Acknowledgments

There are many people without whose help this book could quite possibly have never come into being.

I first want to thank my friend and editor Terry Beswick. Who would have thought that, after nearly coming to blows and expulsion from rehab, we would one day come to work so closely on a project such as this? Bless you for your God-given talents, brother, and thank you for all of the time and effort that you put into this project.

I also want to thank my dear Aunt Rachel Cockrell, who was the third set of eyes on this project from the first page to the last. What a wonder you are, Rachel! Bless you for your keen eye for detail, and for your nonjudgmental Christian faith. The love of God dwells in you, Rachel; you are an inspiration to all who know you.

The third person I want to thank is my friend Douglas McClain, who sat quietly by as I worked diligently on this project and then at the right time came through with a financial blessing that turned this dream into a reality. God is using you, brother.

I also want to thank my grandmother Mary Lester, my dear friend and spiritual counselor Minister Terry Wells and my church family The City of Refuge, United Church of Christ, for your support and encouragement.

To all of you, thank you so much for helping me to tell my story.

CONTENTS

Chapter One:
Introduction

Where to begin?

Who am I kidding? I don't have a clue as to where to begin writing a book about my life. I'm no writer. It's not likely that I'll ever write any great work of fiction or win any literary awards. No, as far as I know I'm not gifted in that way. But I do, like you, have one story to tell, or - in the language that I use today - a testimony.

Yesterday morning, I woke up with an almost overwhelming urge to go to my computer, turn it on, sit down and begin to write this book. What is interesting to note is that prior to 6 o'clock yesterday morning, I don't remember having even so much as a passing thought of taking on a project such as this.

Now you have to understand something right off the top: it is only because of the Lord that I am sitting at this desk right now. Because if anybody else would have come to my bedroom door at 6 o'clock in the morning talking about writing a book, or a letter, or even my name for that matter, I would have questioned their sanity, their sobriety, and possibly their right to live. No - I've learned that when the Lord God says move, I move. "Faith without works is dead." No sense in sitting up arguing with the Lord. He already knows how dumb you think you are. He already knows that I type with one finger. And yes, the Lord our God in heaven, knows every detail of the story I'm about to tell you.

And yet, even with all of that (at times damaging) information, God loves me. I know that today. He loves me, and he loves you in exactly the same way. It doesn't matter if you're a homeless heroin addict or a televangelist. GOD loves us all through the blood of Jesus Christ, our only hope of glory.

I know that some of you may be thinking, "Well, we all know that." But do we really? Or have some of us been robbed? Have we been cheated out of our inheritance? Have we allowed the church to cover the Christ with so much religion and opinion that we really don't even know who Jesus Christ really is, or what our God has done for us all in him?

Well I can only speak for myself. For most of my life I didn't know Jesus; I barely even knew who he was. Oh, I knew the Christmas songs, and I've seen images of the baby in the manger for as many years as I've been alive. I even played one of the wise men in my sixth grade Christmas play. Lord knows I've seen and worn the crosses, but know the Lord? The very best I could say was, "Yes, I believe that there is a GOD... somewhere."

A big part of the problem was the fact that from as far back as I can remember I was homosexual. I'm not talking about finding out during puberty or discovering

2

myself as a teenager or young adult. I'm talking eight or nine years old, I knew that I was gay. That's before I even knew what sex was really. I am convinced that homosexuality is not something that you do; it's something that you are. Now, how would anybody react to a religion that has always seemed to take such exceedingly great pleasure in proclaiming that the "who you are" is sin, plain and simple. I've never seen anything quite like it. I cannot tell you how many times I've been kicking back watching Christian television, hoping to get a word from the Lord or at the very least a word of encouragement, when BAM! Here we go again: "HOMOSEXUALITY IS A SIN! An abomination! God hates fags! Turn or burn!", and on, and on, and on. This usually followed by some cruel joke about some "out" celebrity or the old stand-by, "Adam and Steve." That followed by a rush of laughter and something akin to joy flowing all through the building.

Now I know that emotional cruelty is not funny to me as an adult, but imagine what effect that must have on an eight or nine-year-old child. You expect it from the other kids; after all they're just kids. That bullying spirit sits heavily on our young lives, but what about when it comes from the adults, or even worse, from the pulpit? Try as I might, I know that I won't be able to resist challenging some of those self-righteous, condescending, bullying spirits on the subject of winning the world for Christ.

However, it is not my intention to try to beat up on the Christian church, or the clergy, or even specific persons whom I feel have hurt me and countless other people like me or helped to stunt my spiritual growth.

The fact is we all hurt each other; all of humanity has got "issues" with one another. No, I have no delusions that I'm going to be able to somehow "work it out" or even to "figure it out" in these few pages. Only God himself knows why we act the way we do, and why we treat each other as badly as we do. Just as surely as he knew that he could depend on humanity to brutally murder his only son, God knows us.

No, all I'm going to attempt to do here, reader, is to tell you my story. My prayer is that I will be able to do so without turning this endeavor into a forum for venting all of my hurt, frustration and resentment. Of course some of that is part of my truth. But for me to sit here and try to blame the Christian church, or society, or even the devil himself - although I'm sure that he had a hand in it - for nearly twenty-five years of waste, drug addiction, criminal activity and multiple incarcerations would be much more than a stretch, it would be an out-and-out lie. The truth of the matter is I got hooked on crystal methamphetamine because 1) I tried it; 2) I liked it; and 3) I kept on doing it. Sure, it could be debated that the circumstances of my childhood, my lack of self-worth, and a series of bad choices and decisions might have easily culminated in a "perfect storm" for me to turn to drugs and alcohol. But in all honesty that's just not the way that I remember the story. More like: I went to the party one night and never came back.

In this story, I'm going to tell you about the party, about the dope, the crime, the prisons, and eventually, how and why I believe I got AIDS. All of that of course after I spend a couple of chapters telling you; who I am, and where I came from.

And then there's going to be a shift, Hallelujah! Then I'm going to get a chance to tell you about what I really want to tell you about. About the only thing that brings joy to my soul and deliverance to my mind and body. About a hope alive within me that defies explanation. I'm going to get my big chance to "tell somebody" about my one-on-one, personal encounter with the spirit of Jesus Christ, our Lord and Savior! Oh, yes, he really is good news. And he's good news for everybody, not just those who claim to be the righteous ones.

If I were pushed to liken myself and my spiritual experience to any one character in the Bible, it would have to be the man who was born blind in John 9. After Jesus had healed the man, the "very religious" Pharisees approached him, accusing The Christ of being a sinner because he healed him on the Sabbath. With that, the man began his answer with a simple yet profound truth: "I don't know if he is a sinner or not. All I know is that I was blind, but now I can see!" The key word for me in this simple statement is "know". This man was not in the least bit uncertain about three important points in this statement: First, he knew with absolute certainty that he was born blind. Second, he was just as certain that he could see the people he was standing there talking to. And the third important point in this simple statement is in the way that the man begins: "I don't know if he is a sinner or not." Herein lays yet another difference between religion and faith. This man wasn't the least bit concerned about sin - or what the Pharisees viewed as sin - and neither was Jesus. I would venture to say that after this one encounter with The Son of God, this man who was born blind had something that the religious fanatics would never have. This man "knew" God in the person of Jesus Christ. This kind of knowing was almost certainly based solely on the intimate knowledge that Jesus had done something for him that he knew was impossible.

Is it no wonder that Jesus chose to first strike Saul of Tarsus blind, and then to heal him? He didn't have to do that you know; Jesus was given all power and authority over heaven and earth. He could have called Saul in any way he wanted to. But for some reason, Jesus, with all the wisdom of heaven, chose to first strike Saul blind, then to promise him his sight back, and then to deliver on what he promised. Because Saul was delivered, we now have the teachings of the apostle Paul, and about two thirds of the New Testament. Without ever meeting Paul, I know in my heart that there were many times when he must have taken his mind right back to that Damascus road, back to the place where he first encountered the spirit of Jesus.

Yes, "he whom the Son sets free is free indeed." I'm here to share my experience, and to encourage anyone who might need encouragement right about now: there really is a way out. Jesus said, "I am the Way, the Truth, and the Life." Now was the Son of God talking about being the way out of the crack house here? Or was he talking maybe about being the way out of addiction to internet pornography? Or perhaps, Jesus was talking about being the way to stop beating your spouse? Or the way to stop drinking, or smoking, or shooting heroin, or, or, or... It seems like we just keep coming up with more and more "ors." To all these things and to everything else that crawls on or beneath the earth, I declare that Jesus Christ is the way. The way to what? The way to knowing God, this is the true deliverance, knowing God.

Now, I was at a popular hangout for the recovery community here in San Francisco just last night, when BAM! The enemy attacked! I know that it was him, because he often times shows up in a spirit of fear and self-doubt. "Boy, you can't write no book like that!" he said. "All this talk about Jesus being the way, and making it sound like that's the only way somebody can know God. Listen to what the people are saying." And sure enough, "the thing" was right. (Isn't that just like him to always use just a grain of truth?) Just about everyone in the place was talking about God. Granted, most were using the term "Higher Power," but just think about how many names were given to God in the Hebrew Bible alone. No, there was something going on there last night, something that I was supposed to get. So as I was standing around, by this time deliberately listening to the conversations around me, hearing former drug addicts and alcoholics (many clean now for ten or fifteen years) talking about turning their will and their lives over to the care of God as they understood him, talking about prayer, meditation, and surrender, I thought, "Lord, what about that? You said yourself in John 14:6 that you were... the Way, the Truth and the Life, and that no one could come to the Father without you. Why did you say that, Master? All we do is fight about it here, and what about the Jews, and the Muslims, and the Hindus, and the Buddhists, and all of the other religions of the world? Who's right about you?

Why have so many people around the world throughout history been willing to die for their faith, if most of it means nothing? Shouldn't the Holy Spirit have spoken to all of these misguided souls by now, and told them that Jesus is the only way? I don't understand.

And I've never spoken a truer word, reader. God is far too vast and majestic to fit into any box, book or religion that either you or I would try to fit him into. I'm not going to pretend that I understand the unseen things of God and his purposes. I don't know where he lives or where he came from, any more than I understand why most people are heterosexual, and some people are homosexual. Or why he chose to have so many different races, and allows for so many religions to flourish. No, I'll have to leave all of that kind of talk to the theologians, and the people who have made it their life's work to study the written words. As for me, well, I'm a lot like that blind man in John 9 "All I know is that I was blind and now I can see." Or in my case, all I know for sure is that I was a hopeless drug addict lying in a prison cell waiting to die and now I'm not.

Walk with me; I want to tell you what happened.

Chapter Two:
Easter Sunday, 1958

Well, you can relax reader; I'm not going to try to tie some deep spiritual meaning to the fact that I was born on Easter Sunday. But nevertheless, that's what happened. The way my mother tells it, she was in church praising the Lord when she went into labor.

Mother was seventeen years old and unmarried. We lived in Indianapolis, Indiana. We were, without a doubt, poor, but not much poorer than most black folks at that time. Of course, I was barely aware of what was going on back then, what with being a baby and all. But over the years I must have heard it all at least a hundred times or more.

You see, I'm from one of those big African American families. Grandmother had nine children: five boys and four girls. And of course all of them had children, too. Yes, my grandmother's house was always full of people, and we celebrated everything together: Thanksgiving, Christmas Eve, the Fourth of July and pretty much anything else my grandmother was willing to cook for.

Make no mistake about it - if my grandmother was cookin', everybody was comin'.

To this very day one tradition stands firm in that family: at some point the adults separate and start up a conversation about the good old days and how poor they were. Back then, I never did quite get how they could recall the very worst of economic circumstances, and then identify those days as "the good old days." (I say "they," because this conversation was only for the generation before me. My generation didn't know what poor was. In my family, you had to really *know* poor to *talk* about poor.) So this is the way that I was able to piece together most of what I know about the early beginnings of my life.

Of course, as in most families, there are some things that no one wants to talk about. Isn't it strange how those are the very things I remember best? But I'm getting a little bit ahead of myself here already; I need to go back just a little bit.

When I was a little past my first birthday, my mother got married. You would think that this would be good news, what with her being an unwed mother and all. Mother should have been finishing up high school in 1959; instead here she was eighteen-years-old, with a one-year-old baby and no husband.

I never did get the story straight about my natural father. I do have a vague memory of meeting him, so maybe he stopped by to see me once, before he took off. Mother never once bad-mouthed him, so I figured that they must have just been a couple of teenagers who got in trouble and, according to my mother, on her very first time around. No hard feelings, but no family.

Then, "along came a spider and sat down beside her". If only my mother would have run away. Didn't she know that spiders bite?

Billy Jackson (not his real name) was to be my mother's first husband. Tall, dark, and - I guess many women would say - handsome. A real slickster that Billy Jackson. Dark, dark skin, shiny white teeth, shiny processed hair, shiny shoes, and fingernails. Yeah, I guess you could say that pretty much everything about Billy Jackson was shiny. Everything except for his eyes. There was something about that man's eyes that sends a chill through me even now. If it's true, as they say, that the eyes are the windows to the soul, then Billy Jackson's soul was a dark and scary thing. Maybe that's why he always tried to keep his outsides so shiny.

Billy was from San Francisco, and maybe that was part of the attraction. Maybe my mother saw Billy as her ticket out of Nap Town (Indianapolis) and her current circumstances. Or maybe she really did love him. I don't know what the motivation was, I only know what happened: they met, got married, had a little girl and then off the four of us went to San Francisco, California.

I'm not sure exactly how long after we arrived in California that the beatings started. But start they did. Billy was a cruel and brutal wife-beater. There were probably already danger signals going off long before we left Indianapolis, but there my mother had her five brothers. Now we were over two thousand miles away, living in Billy's hometown. No brothers and no witnesses - at least not any that knew or cared anything about my mother. The gloves came off.

The clearest memory I have about the time we spent in California was of a hellish ride on a Bay Area freeway. We had been visiting with one of my stepfather's relatives when the fight broke out. Of course, in front of the relatives and in their house, there was only yelling and screaming, but we all knew what was coming once we got home.

This time, we didn't make it that far.

Billy was driving fast, really fast, yelling and screaming at my mother, weaving in and out of lanes, driving faster and faster as he got madder and madder. Me and my sister were screaming and crying in the back seat. Suddenly, Billy snapped, lunging at my mother, punching her in the face repeatedly, all the while driving with one hand and weaving back and forth between lanes. Panicking, I opened the back door and was trying to jump out of the fast moving car when somehow one or the other of them must have caught my shirt.

I still remember the details of that nightmarish night forty-three years later.

Of course, the incident and many others like it traumatized me, but I have long since given up trying to figure out exactly how much damage was done to my young psyche by being raised in that environment.

To be sure, whatever it was like for me, it was much worse for my mother. Billy was not into beating children; in fact, I don't even remember ever being spanked by him.

Nevertheless, I could never understand how he could treat my mother the way he did, and still somehow think that we were friends. We were never friends; I hated

Billy Jackson. How could he have not known that I would hate him?

We only stayed in San Francisco for about three years, and in that time, my second little sister was born. How my mother loved that little baby! She and the baby were both what the southern folks would call "high yellow." My first sister looked just like her daddy, and now this new baby looked just like her mother, and our dysfunctional parents chose their favorite accordingly.

Then there was me, Timothy. I was neutral - I didn't remind anybody of anybody.

So after three years of being Billy's punching bag, my mother started planning her escape. But you couldn't just leave Billy Jackson. She/we definitely had to *escape*. If he caught her trying to get away he'd put her in the hospital, or worse.

We couldn't very well go back to Indianapolis; that would be the very first place that he'd come looking for us. No, Indy was definitely out. But there were relatives on my mother's side living in New York, and looking back, I assume Billy knew nothing about them. At any rate, when Billy went to work at the naval shipyards early one morning, as he always did, my mother grabbed her purse, a bag of clothes, her three children, and "hit it." By the time Billy was breaking for lunch, the four of us were sitting on a train headed for New York City. I wouldn't have put it past ol' Billy Jackson to try to catch up with the Greyhound – I wonder if my mother was thinking the same thing when she bought those train tickets.

New York was great. We moved to Long Island. I was six years old. Can't say that I remember much of the city now, but I sure liked those New York relatives. They were so nice to us kids, and it was really great seeing people be nice to my mom too. But of course the best part about being in New York was being away from that monster Billy Jackson!

You can imagine the horror I felt when, a year later, he showed up. Billy was there in New York City with us! Of course the same thing started up again, and again, and before I knew it, we were living back in Indianapolis, and Billy was living with us.

My young mind couldn't comprehend any of this. What was wrong with my mother? Didn't she hate him as much as I did? When was this going to stop?

Was Billy going to kill my mother?

Finally, when I was eight years old, my mother and her husband broke up for the very last time. I could finally exhale. I remember feeling like I had been holding my breath for my entire life. That may sound like a bit of an exaggeration, but to be sure I was never able to totally relax in that house - violence could erupt without a moment's notice. Sure it would have been nice to have a dad around, but I never saw Billy in that way. If there was one thing that I could say that I was proud of as a child, it was that Billy Jackson was not my real father. After the divorce, my mother told me that I could actually change my last name back to what it was before she married him, and I jumped at the chance.

Unfortunately, this reprieve was not to last for very long. Within a year of my mother's split from Billy Jackson, she went and got herself a boyfriend. Can't say that I can blame her much – her marriage had been more like being in a war than a relationship. Theo (not his real name either) must have looked pretty good to my mother. A real nice guy who loved kids, kind of average looking – not flashy and all shiny like Billy. Theo was one of those hard-working types who wore sweatshirts and loved baseball. To look at him, you never would have thought that on the inside, Theo was not much different from Billy Jackson.

Mother was back on the front lines in no time flat. This time, however, her brothers armed themselves, and took turns sleeping at our house. Eventually, Theo decided to move on – but only after three more years of my impressionable youth had been spent walking around on pins and needles.

Maybe if my mother would have just survived a very bad marriage and then was alone for awhile, and then maybe met a different kind of guy somewhere down the line, she would have been fine. But that's just not the way it happened, and my mother was not fine. None of us were. Mother was left bitter and hostile, especially towards men – all men.

And I was the only male around.

As far as my mother was concerned, all black men had the same first name: "nigga." Those few years after she broke up with Theo were hellish. The tiniest little thing would set her off. I had always lived in fear of my mother's men going off on her. Now the tables had turned; now I was the one being beaten.

To make matters worse, it was right around this same time that I started feeling like there was something very different about me – actually, I had been feeling this way for about a year before Theo took off, since I was nine.

Now, I know that the psychological types are going to start analyzing the details of my family dynamics here. But as far as I know, there has never been any connection made between homosexuality and violence in the home.

What is very interesting to me now about this period in my development is that I don't remember it being very sexual. Sure, I messed around a little with the neighborhood kids, but I don't think I did any more than anybody else at that age. I don't think any of us ever actually even touched each other. No, this was something very different from that. This had much more to do with who I was, as opposed to what I did. It's very hard to put this kind of awareness into words, especially nearly forty years after the fact, but all I can do is try.

It wasn't that I was effeminate, but at the same time, I wasn't quite as masculine as the other boys my age either. As I recall, I didn't particularly care for either football or hopscotch. The nickname my family gave me was "timid Timothy." And a truer nickname was never given; I'd cry over just about anything. Whatever the cause, no one could deny that I was an unusually sensitive child.

Another thing that I remember with painful and absolute clarity is the fact that no matter what the other kids would say or do to me, I would never, ever, fight back. The very thought of any kind of violence would send me running for my momma. And boy, how she hated that.

When I was eleven years old, there was another interesting change. Me, my mother and my two sisters packed up and moved into the Emerson Greens Housing Project. As a rule the projects are not a place for a lot of whining and crying. And no one was wanting to hear any of that sensitive kid crap either. Every day on the way to school, I either had to toughen up or get punched in the nose. But what I was amazed to find out was that I could adapt. No, I was never going to convince anybody that I was a tough kid, but boy could I make them laugh. What I discovered at eleven years old was that if I could make people laugh, I could make them like me, and if I could make them like me, they wouldn't want to beat me up. As Richard Pryor once said, "All I had to do was keep 'em laughing."

This was not a bad thing, at the time; I just loved acting a fool. The more I harassed the teachers, the more popular I became. Of course this didn't sit well with the teachers, or with my mother. But I didn't care – no one understood what it was like to be me.

Besides, just as soon as I was old enough, I was going to quit school anyway. I hated it there.

The Emerson Greens were located way out near the edge of town, surrounded by two trailer parks, a cemetery and the State Mental Hospital – talk about your diverse communities.

But the best part about living there was that it was built right alongside of Fall Creek. Me and three close friends must have spent over half of our waking hours in and around that creek. It connected to everything.

One day we followed the creek to the local drive-in theater. As I recall we snuck in, as usual; we were too young to get in legitimately, even if we did have any money. But on this particular day, as we made our way out, a middle-aged white man approached us. Of course we thought we were in big trouble now. He said his name was Ken and that he wasn't a security guard.

Ken was a pedophile.

Out of respect for the other people involved, I'm only going to talk about what happened to me.

This man was some kind of traveling contractor. His *modus operandi* was to seduce his victims slowly - with money, gifts and lots of take-out food. Then, after about two or three weeks, on the night before he was to leave town, he'd make his move. Of course, if anybody did tell or call the cops, he'd be long gone by morning. I can still remember the look on his face when I told him that I thought I might be gay. This pervert was not looking for "gay." What he wanted was my innocence; there was nothing gay about it. Nevertheless, this was my first time having sex to ejaculation, so I guess he got what he wanted. The next day, when we went back, Ken had checked out. And the motel manager told us that the police had been called. We took off, of course, and fast.

I don't know what the full effect of this single encounter was on my young mind. At twelve I was having a ball, playing with my friends in the creek, customizing our bicycles, terrorizing my little sisters – things were finally going well for me.

Then along came this spider.

Because I have no desire to be anything but totally honest here, I have to say that I don't believe that this pedophile had anything to do with me being gay. I was already gay long before he rolled up. I just hadn't had sex yet. No, I think that possibly the worst damage this pervert did to me was that he taught me what it was to ejaculate.

After a boy learns about that, well, it's not like he can just forget about it.

When the guys started going into puberty a couple of years later, I didn't get it. What was the big deal? I had been masturbating since the seventh grade. Since the night it happened.

After three years of living there in the projects, mother got blessed - she bought her own home. It wasn't a big house, but boy was it nice, a lot nicer than living in the projects. The thing about the projects was, when I was a little kid it was great, I had a lot of fun, and I really grew up a lot there.

But now I was thirteen or fourteen and starting to get into some bigger trouble. You see, you had to keep up with what was going on around you, and I felt like this was especially true for me. With every passing day, it seemed like I was becoming more and more aware of my differentness. In order to maintain my status as "one of the boys" I felt like I had to always do more than anybody else. Since I wasn't the least bit inclined towards sports, I found other ways to excel. When we went to the supermarkets, I always stole more than anybody else, same thing with the malls, the lumberyards, and the five-and-dimes. I'd steal anything that wasn't attached to something. Yeah, this was a good time for us to move. I was on the fast track to some real trouble with the law.

And you know what, it worked! From the moment I put the sheets on my new bed in our new home, my life of crime was over. Oh, happy day! How my mother must have rejoiced over signing that mortgage. She had come a long way since her divorce, and in more ways than one. One of the first things she did after we moved was to promise me that she would never hit me again. And she never did.

Of course I was getting to be a very big boy by then – my full six feet by age 13. But still there was something in her eyes that said that she knew that the way she had been treating me was wrong. This was about as close as I was ever going to get to my mother saying, "I'm sorry." I can't say that it was all her fault though; she was already picking me up at the police station when I was eleven. And not only was I stealing everything I could get my hands on around the neighborhood, I had been hitting my mother's pocketbook since I was eight. No – sensitive kid or not, I was no angel. I'm sure that pretty much any single mother would have been somewhat challenged in trying to parent me alone.

And now all of that was behind us. I wonder if somebody was praying for me way back then. Well, that would have had to have been my grandmother – this was many years before my mother found the Lord. Grandmother was always praying for everybody. She was an old-time preacher's kid from the south, and my grandmother had always been in church. Grandmother must have spent more time on her knees before the Lord in those days than most people spent on their feet. As I said, there were a lot of us.

Usually the teenage years are the time for rebellion and mischief. Not so in my case – I had always been rebellious and mischievous, but now I seemed to be conforming. Got my first job at fifteen, right along with my first car and my first girlfriend... Make that my first *and only* girlfriend. My girlfriend Lana (not her real name), now that's an interesting story.

As I sit here today trying with all of my heart to tell the absolute truth, I have to admit that I'm not really sure what the truth was here. There are two possibilities. Either I fell in "puppy love" with Lana (in very much the same way that any other fifteen-year-old boy falls "in love" with a girl for the first time) or – for my own sanity and for appearance's sake – I very much needed to divert attention from this whole gay issue. I suspect that it was probably a little bit of both. I'll be the first to admit that I was probably getting a little paranoid about this whole gay thing right around the time that Lana and I hooked up. Could people tell just by looking at me? I wondered. My mother was always making comments about certain actors on TV having "fag lips." Was she baiting me? Was there something wrong with my mouth?

Well, be that as it may, by the time Lana and I finally got around to attempting to do "the thing," I knew with absolute certainty that I was gay. In fact, I had this revelation while I was still lying on top of her. That would prove to be my first and last attempt at having sex with a member of the opposite sex.

Even though I was no longer getting into a lot of trouble, I was still having issues. For as long as I could remember I had been planning on quitting school, just as soon as I was of age. Well, the legal age to quit school in Indiana was sixteen, and I had been secretly coveting that birthday probably since the day I started kindergarten. Well, maybe not that far back, but pretty close. This became a self-fulfilling prophecy. A little before my sixteenth birthday, I quit. This was to be the beginning of a lifetime pattern – whenever I didn't like something, for whatever reason, I simply quit.

Thankfully, this didn't last however. By the following year, I was back in school. And to everyone's amazement (including mine), this time instead of getting all C's, D's, and F's, I was getting mostly A's and a few B's. All of a sudden, I loved school. Maybe I just needed to prove to myself that I was the one in charge - that I was there because I wanted to be, not because I had to be. Whatever my teenage rationalization, I was back and doing better than anyone ever dreamed I would. I was even making friends again. (There had been a draught since I left my buddies back in the projects.)

The only problem was gym class. It's hard to hide certain things when you're completely naked, and because of this I defiantly refused to go to gym class. No, that does not make me a pervert; I'd like to see how well the straight boys would hold up trying to get dressed in the girl's locker room. No, that was one F that I'd just have to learn to live with. Somewhere down the line I was going to have to figure something out to deal with this though. You couldn't graduate with out passing P.E., and you couldn't take P.E. in your street clothes.

As it turned out, I wouldn't have to figure anything out after all.

This is the way that I remember my first time getting drunk:

When I came back to high school in 1974, I was a little older than my classmates. I had been "held back" once way back in the third grade when we moved back to Indianapolis. And now I had missed a full year of high school. The only good thing about this situation was that I had my driver's license before anybody else. Even more importantly, I was the first dude in my grade to get his own wheels. This, of course, made me instantly popular.

I had just gotten this great big ole '69 Chrysler New Yorker and, one night, five or six of us decided to break that baby in. I can't say that I remember exactly who brought out the alcohol, but that magical night ended when I wrapped that big Chrysler around a tree. One of us was seriously hurt, and the car was totaled. I was seventeen years old and this was already the second car I had totaled.

After the accident I couldn't bring myself to return to school. After all, there was a kid still in the hospital. I was the driver; I was the older one. How could I have been so irresponsible? No one would ever get to ask me those questions; I simply never went back to school. This time really was to be the end of my formal education – and also the end of my drinking, or so I thought.

When I was nineteen I moved out of my mother's house and got myself a little apartment a few blocks away. Almost immediately, I realized that this was not going to be enough. You see, I was never going to fit in that world. In short order my sister was going to be getting married. Then, a little bit further down the road, my other sister would get married. And of course all of the cousins would get married. Then they'd all start having babies, and buying houses. Probably most would go to church together. The men would sit around

23

watching sports. And they'd all laugh and joke and talk about the same things.

But what about me? Where was I supposed to fit into this new African American middle class utopia? Maybe I could run around and help everybody decorate (don't laugh; I was already starting to do that, before I left). Or maybe I could just stay in the closet, and keep pretending that I just hadn't found the right girl yet. Or even better, maybe I could just go ahead and marry some poor girl, knowing full well that I was incapable of loving her – at least not in the way that a person deserves to be loved. No, even then, I thought that would be the very worst thing to do, the cruelest and most selfish thing to do.

No, I was a grown man now (sort of), and it was time for me to get out there and find out where I fit in. Sure, I could have just stayed there in Indianapolis. There are plenty of gay people in Indianapolis, it's not like I was from a small town.

But somehow that simply was not an option for me. The only way I was ever really going to be free was to leave. After I came to that conclusion, there was not any real choosing process. There was only one place on the planet that I had any interest in living.

I was on my way to Los Angeles, California.

Chapter Three:
Hurray for Hollywood

I got a jaywalking ticket just as I was coming out of the Greyhound Bus Station. In town not even fifteen minutes, and already I was talking to the cops.

Was this some kind of omen?

Well, if the Lord was trying to tell me something, I definitely was not listening. I already had way too much on my mind. For one thing, I didn't know a single solitary soul in LA. Second, I had a total of $37 in my pocket. Third, I didn't have a clue where I was going to sleep that night. And fourth, it was raining, and hard!

Oh well, I thought, I already knew it was going to be rough. No sense in whining about it now. First things first – which way is Hollywood?

That was the one thing that I was very clear about. I had no interest in the rest of Los Angeles. I knew exactly where I wanted to be. You see, mixed in with all of my "California dreamin'" was a child-like desire to "make it big" in show business. This just tickles me today, because I can't for the life of me figure out exactly what part of the business I thought I was going to "make it big" in. I couldn't sing; I couldn't dance; I couldn't act; juggle or do magic tricks. No, I was either clinically delusional, or I was trying very hard to convince myself and everybody around me that there was some practical reason behind my need to live in Hollywood.

When I arrived at the corner of Hollywood & Vine in the midst of that rainstorm in the summer of 1977, I couldn't believe my eyes. I didn't even want to get off the bus. This was terrible! I don't know exactly what I was expecting, but it sure wasn't this. Nothing but soaking-wet homeless people, hookers, hustlers, drug addicts, and drag queens.

So this is what Hollywood, Boulevard was off camera, I thought. There was certainly nothing glamorous about it, and that is a gross understatement. Sleazy is the word.

I can still remember walking up and down the Boulevard in the rain that first night, not knowing where I was going, or what I was even doing there, really. What kind of a person just hops on a bus and comes to a place like this with no money and no place to live? I asked myself. It doesn't make sense.

But I never once thought of going back to Indiana. There was no going back. I absolutely had to make it here.

It must have been on my second or third time down the length of the Boulevard that I met Johnny. And believe it or not, it was just that simple: I moved into his apartment that very same night.

Actually there were quite a few people living in Johnny's apartment. They were a band of black, gay Buddhists from Chicago. Not only were they black and gay and Buddhist, they were also entertainers. Their big "claim to fame" was that they hadn't been "gonged" on "The Gong Show."

Their stage routine was very funny, but to me they were just funny people. They all called each other "Miss Thang," or "girlfriend," or "Mary," or just plain "girl." It seemed like every third word was "honey." This took a little getting used to, and yet I found it not only very funny, but a reasonable act of rebellion. Man, how I would chuckle when I was introduced to people like "Miss Fred" or "Miss Charles." These guys were hysterical to me; they seemed to elevate camp to an art form.

So in my first couple of hours in Hollywood I had gotten lucky. Things could have gone a lot differently – I would have done anything to stay in LA.

After the first couple of days, my opinion of Hollywood, Boulevard changed dramatically. Whereas at first glance it had somewhat resembled a cesspool, now it appeared to be the most exciting place on Earth. It sure makes a difference, I guess, knowing where you're going to sleep at night. That, plus the rain had stopped.

This was the beginning of a very exciting time for me, a time of self-discovery and exploration. And I was not alone. There were hundreds, if not thousands, of young people like me everywhere I looked. This was a whole lot different than the three or four gay people I could identify at my high school who I wouldn't even so much as speak to for fear of guilt-by-association. Finally I didn't have to hide or be ashamed. Not anymore.

This, I thought, was the place where I would build my life.

It was after just a couple of months at Johnny's place that I met my first celebrity. Actually, this guy didn't have a lot of *personal* celebrity, but boy, what a client list he had. He was a costume designer, and through him I actually got to see some of the glamorous side of Hollywood. I had only been in town two or three months and already I was meeting and sometimes holding conversations with practically every R&B singing group that I had ever listened to! This was pretty heady stuff for a nineteen-year-old boy fresh off the bus from Indiana. For a while there it just seemed like I could do no wrong. This guy even helped me to get my own apartment. I lived right off of the Boulevard, almost directly behind Mann's Chinese Theater.

I couldn't have asked for a better first year in Los Angeles. I was having a very good time.

I should note here that up to this point I had had no need or desire to do drugs. I had gotten drunk a couple of times in Indiana (most notably, the time that I wrecked the Chrysler.) And I had smoked pot occasionally, if it was offered to me. But I don't remember ever having had a desire to get high, and I certainly never went out and bought drugs on my own.

My designer friend and his crowd smoked a lot of pot, and because I spent pretty much every weekend up at his house for over a year, there was plenty of opportunity and unlimited supply, but still it didn't really take. Drugs were just not that big a deal for me. I was still getting high on just being in LA, and on being there on my own. Besides, every time I smoked pot I fell asleep. Sleeping all day was the last thing I wanted – I didn't want to miss anything.

All of that was about to change.

When I was almost twenty-one, I met my first "lover." (That was the language of the day. Today we would have been called "partners" – maybe soon that word will change again. But in the late seventies, the only term used to describe two men who loved each other and lived together was "lovers.")

David and I met at the Hollywood Spa. This was a few years before the AIDS epidemic hit the U.S., so at that time the bathhouses were still an integral part of the gay experience. You couldn't get into the bars and discos until you were twenty-one, but you only had to be eighteen to get into a bathhouse. David was a twenty-year-old white guy with a huge blonde Afro. No, there was nothing "ethnic" about him – he just had very long, very curly, bleached-blonde hair, which he picked out for maximum effect.

We were together from the very first day we met.

David had been around the gay scene a lot longer than I had, even though we were both not yet twenty-one. The way he told it, he had always been out. He simply was not the kind of kid that could hide it. His parents had kicked him out of the house at fourteen, and he had basically been on the streets or in foster care ever since. I found him kind of sad, kind of tragic, and very easy to love.

David was also a drug addict. Mostly it was pot and tequila around the time that we met, but that man would drink, snort, pop or smoke just about anything he got his hands on to stay high. And it didn't take long for me to catch up with him. Smoking pot was always the first thing we did in the morning and the very last thing we did at night. Whereas it used to put me right to sleep, now it was the reason that I got up in the morning. In fact, if there was no pot in the house to wake up to, I simply would not go to bed at all, and instead I would prowl around the streets of Hollywood all night – which is where I stumbled into my next line of work.

I was naive, yes, but not so naive that I didn't know that there was money to be made as a male prostitute. In fact, if the truth be told, that had been my back-up plan ever since the day I left Indianapolis. But somehow I had just never been able to bring myself to actually do it. There never seemed to be any real need to do it. After all, I had gotten quite a bit of help since I got to town. But that was different – those guys knew what I needed and just gave it to me. I didn't ask them for anything. Besides, people like the designer guy had plenty of money, and they liked spending it. It's only natural, I suppose, to want to help young people.

But now I was contemplating actually getting in cars with strangers and having sex in exchange for money. In my right mind, I couldn't have brought myself to do it. But I wasn't in my right mind anymore. I was high all the time. And being high all the time took cash.

Fortunately for me, David absolutely despised prostitution. As a kid living on the streets of LA, he'd had to do it just to survive. He knew the life well – too well – and there was no way that I was going to be with him, he said, and be out there turning tricks.

We fought about it a lot, and after a while I gave it up. It helped that David had come up with another more brilliant idea: he got a job.

Looking back, of course, it seems like getting a job should have been a given, especially for someone with my background, where everybody over the age of sixteen worked somewhere, at least part-time. And trust, as soon as school was out, you had to go out and get a real job, man .We all knew that scripture: "If a man don't work, he don't eat," right?

Well, that might be what was right, but let me tell you, I for one had absolutely no interest in working for a living. I was having way too much fun. Had I come all the way out to California just to get a job? To work eight or ten hours somewhere, come home, eat dinner, watch a movie, and go to bed? I could have done that in Indiana.

Besides, when would I have time to get high with a schedule like that?

No, working was definitely out, but I still needed money. You see, David and I had come to an uneasy (and for the most part unspoken) agreement. Basically, he worked and paid most of the bills, while I supplied the drugs. This arrangement was not nearly as unequal as you might think, since our drug bill far exceeded our living expenses. By this time we were doing copious amounts of LSD, MDA, Quaaludes, Black Beauties, Angel Dust, Mescaline, alcohol and weed.

Actually, David was doing most of the drinking; at that point I hated the taste of alcohol. How that dude ever made it to work every morning I'll never know. He did manage to lose quite a few jobs, but he never stopped trying. He'd lose a job one week, and then a couple of weeks later he'd be working someplace else. That was David's hustle.

As for me, I did a lot better in the streets. At first it was enough to just sell joints and dime bags of weed on the Boulevard, but before long I was back to doing what I did so well as a kid back in the projects. Once again I found myself back in the department stores. Only this time, I wasn't stealing for kicks or status – this time I was in it purely for the money.

So that's the way that my first lover David and I lived for the remainder of our relationship. He'd go to work every morning, and I'd go out stealing. Of course, I had to open up shop at night to fence all of my loot and to barter with the drug dealers. "Boosting" was a double-edged sword: first you had to acquire the merchandise, and then you had to turn it into cash or drugs. Most of the time, if I couldn't get the money directly from the stores, I had to barter the merchandise for drugs and then sell some of the drugs for cash.

This was a lot of activity going on under one roof, and of course before long resentment and tension started building between us. You see, all David got for going to work every day and trying to do what most people would consider "the right thing" was a pay check. I, on the other hand, was becoming very popular and actually thriving in this new criminal persona I had taken on. Whenever the phone rang, it was for me. If there was a knock at the door, it was for me. If someone dropped a "package" off, it was always for me. Before long our apartment seemed more like a 7-11 store than a place where people lived. The only time the doorbell was for him, it was the landlord looking for the rent.

Of course, inevitably, all of my money was tied up in the drugs.

The icing on the cake was when I started going to jail. Not only did this leave David alone and feeling abandoned, it instantly cut off his seemingly endless supply of dope.

This was an impossible situation. It was like trying to mix oil and water. And it was about to get much worse.

David and I had just turned twenty-one – he in March and me in April. We had been able to sneak into the bars a little here and there before this, but the law and the bar owners were very strict about carding. (This was especially true in dealing with black folks. Oh, yes, we were all gay, but we were not all the same – at least not on that playing field. The majority still ran everything, and I was about to learn some very harsh and painful realities about life in my new so-called community, and about human nature in general. But I'll get back to that.) David and I started pouring alcohol onto this already smoldering flame of resentment burning into our dysfunctional relationship.

I know that somewhere long ago, society decided that alcohol is okay and drugs are not. But I have to tell you that the effects of alcohol on our relationship – and on me personally – far exceeded anything I had ever experienced while under the influence of any drug. Whereas marijuana, pills and especially LSD were making me lazy, stupid, anti-social, paranoid, and pretty useless to anyone except people in the same condition, alcohol took me over the top. And "the top" for me would always be some form of violence.

I had always hated violence in other people, but now I was finding out that I absolutely despised it in myself. Previously, I hadn't even thought myself capable of hitting or kicking another human being, least of all someone that I cared about.

Little did David know that after our very first fist fight, our days together would be numbered. The one person on this planet that I was not going to become was Billy Jackson.

Figuring out how to end the relationship was not going to be hard. David came home one night flying high on acid, alcohol and I don't know what else (probably Angel Dust, too, because he was as strong as a bull). Whatever it was, it took him way, way, over the top. David went into a rage the likes of which I hadn't seen since my childhood, breaking and smashing everything in sight, clawing and screaming like a wild animal. I didn't know what to do; there was broken glass everywhere. I knew somebody was going to be hurt badly if I didn't do something!

Suddenly, it came to me. I rushed David, picked him up and literally threw him out the front door, and locked it. Fortunately, there were no front windows to the apartment, but he tried to kick down the door.

And then, nothing – David was gone. He must have heard the sirens.

This was to be the way that my first real relationship ended. However, there was still one last bizarre scene to be played out.

On the very same night that David took off running from the cops, he got on a bus headed for San Francisco. I got a couple -barely legible- letters from him there. I could tell that he was really drugged out. After all, he had worked as a secretary, and I couldn't even make out his handwriting.

David had messed up bad, but I felt absolutely horrible about the way things had turned out. After all, who was I to throw him out of his own apartment? He had certainly paid more rent there than I ever had. No, what I had done was not right. Even if he did do too many drugs one night and lose it – who was I to judge? That's all we ever did together, drink and do way too many drugs.

So he could come back, I told him, but our relationship was over. The plan was that David would move back to LA, get on his feet and then either one or both of us would move out and get our own apartment.

When he got back to LA, David was a fright. He looked like he hadn't been asleep since he left town two months earlier. His face was skeletal, and his eyes were ringed with deep dark circles. We were just twenty-two-year-old boys at the time, but David looked to be twice that. And when he unpacked his duffel bag, I instantly understood why. There were literally hundreds of tiny little purple pills in different places all through his stuff. I had never seen so much acid in my entire life. I guess it was true that the hippies were still alive and well in San Francisco.

Of course we had to celebrate David's return to Hollywood. He could always sleep tomorrow, right? As I started to put one of these tiny purple pills into my mouth, he caught my hand. "No, much better to put it in hot tea," he said, and he went into the kitchen to prepare the magic elixir. Imagine the absolute terror that ran through me when I got to the bottom of the teacup, and saw that there were seven of the tiny pills resting in the bottom. This was not going to be good. The pills themselves were not acid; liquid LSD was poured over the hard pills. I had just taken seven hits of acid! In all the times I had taken this drug, there was never even one instance where I had taken more than one pill or tab.

Had I just been murdered? I wondered. Was this the real reason he had come back – for revenge?

But this was no time to be having bad thoughts. I only had fifteen to thirty minutes before all hell was about to break loose in my head. And break loose it did. To this day, that night rates in the top five of the worst nights of my entire life.

Needless to say, I had some serious trust issues with David after that. Was he dangerous? That was my primary concern.

Because he was still there the next day, and in the weeks and months to come, I must have bought his story. He did make one very good point: he had drunk from the very same cup that hellish night, and nothing had happened to him. What kind of a drug tolerance was this? I felt like I had just returned from the outer limits, while he thought that the stuff was so weak that it took seven pills just to feel anything.

Whatever my concerns about David and his motives, they would have to take a backseat. There had been several changes made on the home front since that fateful night that he went running off to San Francisco. One, I had gotten a roommate to help out with the rent. Two, I had finally broken down and gotten myself a job (can you believe it?). And three, I had met Jimmy, the man who would prove to be my one experience with love.

But the drama was not over. Not by a long shot.

Chapter Four: Alcoholic

Jimmy came into my life in the summer of 1980. I was twenty-two and he was twenty-nine – that's quite a difference in "gay years." I won't say that it was love at first sight, but there was something significant that moved between us -- right before he passed out.

We met at The Rusty Nail, West Hollywood's one and only interracial hangout. That's not to say that there weren't black folks hanging out in the other bars; in most, there were usually three or four of us. Yeah, that's about right – three or four black guys and one to two hundred whites. Now, I'm not suggesting that this meant that the entire community of West Hollywood was racist, but it did cater overwhelmingly to white men seeking the company of other white men.

The Rusty Nail was different. This was a bar that (at least in 1980) marketed itself to black men who were into whites and to white men who were into blacks. The Nail was where David and I had gone whenever we went out. And it was there that I met my second lover, Jimmy.

When I look back over my life, even today, I believe that Jimmy is the only person I ever really loved.

We went home together that first night and we had what I thought was a good and memorable time. Two weeks later, however, when I ran into him again, he didn't even know who I was. As it turns out, when we'd met he'd been in the middle of an alcohol-induced blackout. So what could I do? I let him pick me up "for the first time" all over again.

A mild-mannered bank teller by day, Jimmy was a rip-roaring alcoholic by night. He was the kind of a guy who would sit on a barstool until either he fell off, or the bartender cut him off. That was how Jimmy drank.

When he wasn't drinking, Jimmy was a kind and gentle, generous and loving, spirited guy. In fact, Jimmy wasn't a *bad* guy when he drank, either – just what you might call *sloppy*. And man, oh man – did that dude have a roaming eye!

Jimmy had been a heroin addict as a teenager, but at the time we met he was eight years clean (at least from heroin). Coming from all that, I guess he saw his drinking as child's play, and I suppose he had a point, in a way. I mean, everybody drinks – right? Besides, how could you be gay if you didn't drink? The bars were the social center of our world.

Jimmy thought it hysterical that I could actually get falling-down drunk on just three drinks. He, on the other hand, would arrive at the bar at about eight, locate a stool with a view, place two packs of cigarettes on the counter and then sit there and drink until the lights came up.

This didn't happen every night however. Jimmy may very well have been in denial about his alcoholism, but on one point he was very clear: after he started drinking, he couldn't stop, and in the adult world, bills still had to be paid. So both of us had to somehow get up and make it to work Monday through Friday. For that reason, and that reason alone, most of our partying took place on the weekends.

And that was okay by me, just as long as I still had my old stand-by – I was still smoking weed every single day, and taking LSD or MDA whenever I could.

Jimmy, on the other hand, hated all drugs. Heroin had almost killed him. In fact, it *had* killed his mother, who died of an overdose when he was twenty-one, and he had been clean ever since. If there was one single thing that Jimmy did not like about me, he absolutely hated the fact that I liked to get high. Of course alcohol was different.

I'm not sure why I found Jimmy so fascinating in the beginning. Maybe it was because he was older and seemed to know so much more about everything than I did. Or maybe it was the way he lavished so much attention on me – I had never experienced that. David and I had been just boys, and we "loved" each other the way boys do. But Jimmy was a man, and soon I was falling in love with him. He was falling too, a little slower than me perhaps, but falling nonetheless.

So this is what it felt like, I thought. How could the world hate us for this? What could be more natural…. for us?

Meanwhile, things were getting a little crowded at home. First, there were Jimmy and I, who wanted very much to be together all the time. Then there was David, my ex, who still had some lingering idea that we were somehow going to work things out. And finally there was Levi, the roommate that had moved in, taking David's place. And all of this in a one-bedroom apartment.

Of course, Jimmy and I could have and should have waited a while before trying to live together. He was still quite a ways off from making any real commitment, and in this way at least, Jimmy fit one of the oldest stereotypes about gay men.

Very early on, I began noticing that he seemed to know pretty much every black man at the Rusty Nail. Why, I wondered, did they all seem to have something to whisper in his ear? Then there were the phone calls taken in the other room, with the door closed. Then my friends started telling me things. Of course, to me it was all malicious gossip and I didn't want to hear it. "They're all just jealous," I thought, "because I have somebody and they don't!"

Oh well, just because the people were gossiping about it didn't mean that it wasn't true. And after I walked in on Jimmy and David in bed together, it was ridiculous to deny it anymore.

This was no accident. I already knew that David had a dark and vindictive side. But what in the world was Jimmy's problem? Surely he knew how much this would hurt me. Back then, we used much harsher terms, but today Jimmy would probably be considered a sex addict. That's among the more sensitive and compassionate circles. To the rest of us he would still be considered a ---- well let's just say "a very promiscuous person."

This didn't make him a bad guy necessarily; in fact in the gay world it didn't even make him an unusual guy. But relationship material? Any rational person would have seen the signs and headed for the hills. But I wasn't a rational person, I was twenty-two.

A series of circumstances left Jimmy in need of a place to live, so I of course had to take him in – after all he was my boyfriend. David still hadn't gotten on his feet. Levi had come to my rescue when David had taken off, so I couldn't just throw him out on the street. And that's the way that the four of us came to live in the same one bedroom apartment. Of course this would never work, especially after that stunt David had pulled, which naturally had been blamed on the alcohol. But of course, I was just too naive and immature to understand this, and Jimmy never seemed to tire of reminding me: "Tim, we are not lovers, and we are both free to do whatever – and whomever – we want to."

Well, that was just great and oh-so-convenient for him. But I was not a sex addict, and I did not think it strange to expect monogamy between two people who claimed to love each other.

I was coming to realize that there were certain aspects of this new carefree gay lifestyle that I despised.

Adding to my troubles, I knew that David was by no means finished. He would never rest until he had finished breaking us up. How foolish of me to believe that the three of us could share the same space, even temporarily.

It wasn't long before we were all evicted for lack of payment of rent, and for our outrageous behavior. Can you believe it? Four grown men living in a one-bedroom apartment, and we still couldn't pay the rent.

Now I needed an apartment and a roommate, and Jimmy needed an apartment and a roommate. Rents were high in LA even back then – too high to get a place on my own. So Jimmy and I were faced with a decision: dare we try to live together?

No one thought it made any sense. Granted we were calling ourselves boyfriends, but there was no real commitment. Jimmy loved his carefree and promiscuous lifestyle, and it was all out in the open now. I had even learned to pretend that I liked sleeping around, which of course was a humongous lie – I only wanted to be with him. But I was not about to humiliate myself and let him know that.

Still, we both absolutely loved each other's company. I got Jimmy's humor and he got mine. We laughed about all of the same things. I found him an irresistible companion. Sometimes, he seemed to understand me better than I understood myself. If ever there was a relationship based on laughter and companionship, it must have been ours.

So we did it. Jimmy and I got an apartment together, a really nice apartment right in the heart of West Hollywood (LA's gayest neighborhood). On the surface it looked like we were a pretty happy couple of guys. We even got a doggie. But just under the surface, we both understood that we were living in a glass house, and at the first sign of trouble this whole facade was bound to come crumbling down on our heads.

Part of Jimmy wanted to stay home and play house with me, and the other part still wanted to be Peter

Pan, inasmuch as he never wanted to grow up. For my part, I was probably just as fickle. One day I'd want to stay with him and somehow work out our problems, especially our problems around monogamy. And then the very next day, I'd want to be done with the whole charade so that I could get on with the business of finding a good man. Surely every gay man in the city of Los Angles wasn't a ----- (very promiscuous person).

The booze helped – at least at first it did. In fact, we were practically living in the bars. I mean that both figuratively and literally. We lived within a block of six gay bars, and I was a regular in every one of them. But Jimmy preferred the scene back in the old neighborhood. He also preferred to go there alone. Even if we didn't drink together very often, we certainly did everything else as a couple. This was all very confusing for me. I mean, were we "in a relationship" or not? I can remember being paranoid about people laughing at me, especially at our only mutual hangout, The Rusty Nail. Looking back on it now, I can see that I probably wasn't paranoid at all. More than likely they really were laughing at me, especially the ones that were sleeping with my boyfriend.

One day, I came home from work to find that Jimmy had moved out. I guess he'd finally had enough of me calling him a whore. That and the fact that I know that he really did care for me. The guilt that he must have felt over the way things had turned out had to be eating him alive. Rather than drag out the inevitable, he simply chose to leave.

I can't say that I was really all that torn up over his decision either. Sure, I cried that first night when I discovered that his clothes were no longer hanging in the closet. But the very next day, my old roommate Levi moved in, just like he had when David took off for San Francisco. And then, not two weeks after that, I went and got myself another boyfriend.

When Jimmy found out that this guy had moved in to what just a few weeks ago had been our apartment, he went ballistic. "What kind of a person are you?" he demanded. "How could you have moved this creep into 'our' apartment? How could you actually be living with somebody else just three weeks after we broke up?" Who knows; maybe I was just playing mind games. But if that was the case, it must have been on a very subconscious level. As far as I was concerned, Jimmy and I really were "toast." And this new guy – whatever his name was – was my new beau. After all, Jimmy was the one who chose to leave.

Maybe none of the people involved were very clear on each other's motives, but whatever was going on, it worked. A week later, Jimmy was back and lover boy was now "toast." Jimmy and I were now officially lovers. I've got to hand it to him – he really did make pretty close to a one hundred and eighty-degree turnaround; suddenly Jimmy and I were a committed couple. The dog was finally being properly parented. And I'd have to say that, in a general way, we were happy.

The problem was we drank.

Within the first year of our new life together, I had totally caught up with his drinking. It wasn't like I was trying to become an alcoholic because he was an alcoholic. Frankly, I preferred drugs. But the more I got caught up in the bar scene, the more I drank. And the more I drank, the more I got caught up in the bar scene. Drinking and going out just seemed to me to be what gay life was all about.

I wasn't the only person that felt that way; the gay bars around West Hollywood – and all over Los Angeles for that matter – were always packed. Before long I was drinking pretty much every night. The nights that I didn't go out, it was either because I was broke or because I simply needed to rest. Of course I only needed to rest so that I would be ready for the weekend.

The bars were for weekdays and all of my weekends were spent at the discos. I don't know if I was more hooked on going out every night or on the booze itself. For me, there was never any separation – every time I had a drink, I was in a bar. In fact, Jimmy and I never had so much as one bottle of alcohol or even a beer in the apartment.

It's really pretty amazing, when I think about it, that we managed to stay together as long as we did. It was towards the end of our third year together that things started spinning out of control. I didn't like being drunk so much anymore. At first it had been a lot of fun. I'd get really friendly, laugh really loud, tell lousy jokes and lies until "last call for alcohol." But after only three years the alcohol started affecting me differently. Whereas before I had been generally considered (by most people) a happy drunk and a pretty darned nice guy, now I was becoming more and more sarcastic, as well as bitter, obnoxious, angry, paranoid and just downright mean. Even I absolutely hated the way that I would get after a few drinks, and yet somehow I couldn't seem to stop it. I tried taking caffeine pills, and later various kinds of amphetamines, all in an effort to not get quite so drunk. But after a while this only made things worse. Mixing amphetamines and alcohol only made me a wide-awake drunk – and just as mean as a scorched alley cat.

None of this was the reason that Jimmy and I finally broke up, however. No, the beginning of the end came for us when I started noticing bruises on his body.

Oh, God! This was too much. Wasn't it enough that I was born black, and poor, had no father, and gay. Did this mean that I would always be alone too? Oh, God! This was not fair! Didn't I already have nothing?

At that time I was far too ashamed to tell anybody – even Jimmy – about my real beginnings, or about all of the domestic violence that I witnessed as a small child. But when I saw those bruises on his arms and stomach and realized that I didn't even remember hitting him, it was like being back in that house with Billy Jackson all over again – except this time, I was Billy. I knew I would rather be dead than to become what my stepfather was. Intuitively, I knew that things would only get worse.

Thankfully, Jimmy moved out again, and the very next day I went to Alcoholics   Anonymous.

The first time I tried to get clean and sober I was twenty-five years old. Jimmy and I had just broken up, and I was hurting bad. Not only was I giving up alcohol, drugs, my beloved bar scene and Jimmy. I was also being evicted--again!

There was a thriving, clean and sober gay community in and around West Hollywood back in 1983. There were even a few black people – four, if I recall correctly. But I could be wrong – there may have been as many as five of us. But in all honesty, at that time in my life I actually preferred being around all white folks. My unresolved issues around race and culture were numerous, legion you might say. And adding to this dilemma, after I started getting high, I stopped growing up. After all, what was the point? Why should I have to work through my problems, educate myself, seek help or guidance? It was so much easier to just take something, or drink something, or smoke something –so much easier to feel nothing.

My first experience with Alcoholics Anonymous was a very good one. I was one of those people who just loved to go to meetings. Finally, I had found a place where I could actually discuss my problems. Finally, a place where I could rediscover myself and begin to unravel all of the junk that I had been suppressing and medicating for all of my young life. It was through listening to all the personal stories that I listened to night after night that I began to realize that I wasn't so different after all, that I experienced both joy and sorrow pretty much the same way other people did. What I was amazed to find out was that I had experienced many of the same challenges in life that other dysfunctional people had.

No doubt about it, AA was great for me, but giving up drugs and alcohol forever was no simple matter. No wonder so much emphasis was put on doing it "one day at a time." The very idea of never getting high again was enough to send me into a panic attack. Granted, I was at an all time low when I stumbled into the doors of Alcoholics Anonymous. And granted I had probably never been as happy or content in my entire life until after I started going to meetings. But my drinking and drugging were by no means over. Not by a long shot.

My primary stumbling block back then was my age. I just couldn't seem to get around feeling like I was missing out on something, like I was giving it all up way too early. After all I was only twenty five years old when I got clean. In fact, my whole using career from beginning to end had lasted a total of five years. The old timers used to say, "I spilt more on the counter than you drank." After a while I started to wonder if maybe they might not have a point. Maybe I wasn't a real alcoholic after all. Maybe I could just blame this whole thing on Jimmy. After all, wasn't he the one who had been making me so bitter and hostile? No one could deny the fact that I had come to my first meeting the day after he moved out. Funny, all of the things your mind will come up with when you want to drink. But be that as it may, after my third or fourth relapse, the verdict was in: I was indeed alcoholic, and Jimmy had nothing to do with it.

Somehow, I managed to stay clean for about two and a half of the next three years. My "program," if you could call it that mostly consisted of going to AA and NA meetings every day. I will never be able to honestly say whether twelve-step groups would or would not have worked for me. The very term "twelve-step" implies that there are twelve steps to be taken. I never really got past step one.

Still, on the surface things seemed to be going well for me. I had a pretty decent job, my own apartment, and I was positive that I was HIV negative. This latter thing I could surmise only because I had somehow managed to go two full years without any sexual contact at all. Besides, LA was the last of the big cities to be hit by HIV. (Or was it? This was only my perception, based on the conversations I was having at the time.) I believe that at first many of the men in recovery felt like we had gotten lucky, that we had gotten clean just at the right time. After all, none of us were using, or drinking, or sleeping around like we used to. We all had the presence of mind to wear condoms and stay away from the bathhouses. I, for one, felt like my own chances of contracting this new virus were pretty close to nil.

And then people started getting sick. The very first person I knew who died from AIDS had been clean and sober for six years.

These were terrifying times for me and for everybody that I knew. Especially when the media started talking about incubation periods of up to several years, how could anybody really feel safe, whether they were clean or not? Every cold, flu, blister, everything and anything was suspect. Fear had gripped our community. To make things worse, we didn't even have the benefit of knowing exactly how this thing was spreading.

There was lots of talk going around about drug use, and about one drug in particular. As it turned out, this was one of the few drugs that I hadn't gotten around to when I was out there. Apparently many of the people who were getting sick around the program were former crystal methamphetamine users.

I do remember hearing about crystal meth back when I was still "partying," but frankly it was just too expensive for a guy like me. I couldn't even conceive of the idea of paying forty American dollars for a few tiny granules of anything. No, speed was just a means by which I could stay awake and drink all night. The kind of amphetamines I was taking cost only two or three dollars a pill.

Now here I was being inundated with all of this information about this other epidemic that I barely even knew existed. And it's not all that surprising that I didn't hear much talk about this particular drug around the bars. Crystal wasn't nearly so much about going out as it was about staying in. The common denominator between crystal meth and AIDS was two-fold: 1) It was about using needles, and 2) It was about sex – lots and lots of sex. While it was true that not everybody that used meth used needles, it became apparent to me that virtually every gay man that used crystal meth had outrageous amounts of sex. I know that this kind of generalization is likely to tick some people off, and I will have to concede that this was the perception of a man who hadn't had sex at all in over two years. This was not a condition that I willingly chose to be in. Frankly, I was both sexually frustrated in the extreme and paralyzed with fear of AIDS at the same time.

Now you would think that this early association between crystal and AIDS would serve as the ultimate deterrent. And you would be right to think that. Any rational person would be thinking along those lines, but rational thinking had never been one of my strong suits. Still, I believe that because I was clean and in my right mind "most of the time," I didn't just run out and try crystal meth so I could get laid. At least it didn't happen that quickly.

I wasn't the only one having brain trouble; Jimmy was back on heroin. I should have known that he was in trouble when I heard that he started hanging out with this known junkie shortly after we broke up. He had been off of smack for over eleven years.

How could this have happened?

His using again after all those years was by no means the worst part of the news, however. The very worst part was when his using partner became the second person that I knew to die from AIDS.

Jimmy and this guy had shot up and shared needles practically every day.

Another unfortunate series of events found me in urgent need of a place to live... Okay! I was being evicted again. I had learned to keep a job, and I no longer used drugs or alcohol, but I had yet to master the art of paying my bills. So here I was sleeping on Jimmy's couch. The two of them would be locked away in the bathroom shooting up heroin and plotting their next scheme to get more money. And I'd be in the living room reading my AA Big Book. Of course this whole scenario made no sense. I had no business being there.

Before long I was back hanging out with my old friends. Jimmy's friend got very sick, and soon after that, he died. Not long after that, Jimmy was in jail for petty theft and possession of heroin. And then, once again, the landlords were banging on the door. This time I didn't just find another place to crash.

This time I got loaded.

At first, I just walked into a bar on my lunch break and ordered a beer. But then – you guessed it - the first chance I got, I bought my very first bag of crystal methamphetamine.

A monster is born...

Chapter Five: Meth Monster

It is an awful thing when a person is reduced to defining their life by the drugs they take. But that is exactly what meth did for me. Try as I might, there is simply no way for me to minimize the impact with which crystal meth slammed into my life, at least not without straying far from the truth. It was like throwing a forty-pound sledge hammer though a plate glass window.

Mind you, I was not going into this thing totally blind. I had been coveting this drug and obsessing about this drug for a full two years before I got around to actually trying it.

Of course, in the beginning it wasn't such a bad thing. No, to the contrary, in the beginning crystal meth seemed like the best thing that had ever happened to me.

Three or four days after I relapsed on alcohol, I found myself at a big dance bar in Hollywood. It was the weekend of the Gay Pride Parade and the atmosphere was especially festive. I had been drinking every night since the day that I gave up my sobriety, and by Sunday morning I was very, very drunk. This particular bar was known for its all-day "beer bust" which started promptly at 6 a.m. every Sunday morning. It was also the easiest place to find meth.

And that's where it all began. I was already drunk and obnoxious, so what the hell? I just walked up to the first dude I saw who looked like he was dancing a little too fast for the music, and the next thing I knew, we were sitting in his car doing the deal. And then, not ten minutes later, when I walked back into the bar, I had a sudden realization: I was no longer drunk. Just like that, I was in full control of my mind and all of my senses.

There was another thing that I think was very significant about this "maiden voyage" into the underworld of meth. From across the dance floor, I spotted this really attractive young guy leaning over a balcony up above the smoke and the crowd, and I thought, "This has to be the most attractive dude in the place." And do you know what I did? I walked right over to him and I introduced myself. And when we finally left that bar, we left together. Now you would probably have to be me to understand that I could never have done that on my own, even with the help of alcohol. My fear of rejection had always been so intense that I rarely approached anybody.

So what was this? Where was the fear?

It sounds ridiculous even to me if I suggest that a person can be totally hooked on a drug from the very first time that they use it. So let me see if I can put it a different way...

Nope, there is no better way to put it. I was hooked on meth from the very first time I used it. "Hooked", because I could not stop using it after that first morning at the bar. That first day I spent ten bucks. The next day it was eighty. And by the third day, I was back in the department stores, stealing to support my high.

I want to digress here for a moment. Because, if there is one thing that I don't want to do, it is to spark anyone else's curiosity about this or any other drug. To this day I still struggle with the fact that I first heard about crystal meth in 12-step meetings. But I believe that the Lord is calling on me to tell the whole truth and I intend to do just that. So if you are a person who is still struggling to stay sober, or if all of this drug talk simply makes you uncomfortable, then hey, please turn the page, man/woman. That's what I would do. Ultimately, this book is about getting off drugs, after all – not getting on them!

That being said, those early party days on meth were admittedly a lot of fun. It seemed like I just literally danced right through the first few months. And then, just like with alcohol, there was a shift.

That's the thing about what I call "drug demons." At first they just seem to do so much for you. And then, after they get you under their power, it's you that will do anything for them. One minute I was spinning around on the dance floor, just as free as an eagle in flight. And then, in what seemed like just the blink of an eye, I found myself sitting on the floor of a cockroach-infested, abandoned building, trying to find a vein. But in fact, my flight from the dance floor to the nasty floor took about a year.

I was still doing the club scene when I started going to jail. Way back when I was with David I went to the county jail a few times, but now I was going all the time. I was what you would call a petty criminal at that time, and when I was arrested, ninety percent of the time it was for shoplifting. The whole thing had gotten a lot more desperate. At first I just needed enough money to score one time. Then I would sell and barter what little I had to get more and more dope until I went to sleep three or four days later. Soon I couldn't sell any drugs – I was doing it all myself. And after I started shooting up, the "party" was essentially over. I didn't have time to be standing around in clubs. I needed 100 dollars a day minimum to stay high. And as I began stealing more, jail became a second home. With each stint in jail, I came out knowing more and more of what I considered to be the "real" drug addicts: these were easily identifiable speed freaks. Many picked at there skin, wore dirty clothes, and for some reason always seemed to be looking for something on the ground.

There was still a lot of pretense, a lot of "acting as if" around the club scene. True, many guys still had jobs, cars and apartments. But many more were just pretending they did. I know that a lot of those guys were shooting up crystal just as much as I was, but talking about using needles was definitely taboo. The thing was, as long as you looked like you were holding it together you could still find people who would give you drugs.

For me, the final split between these two worlds came after a five or six-day run with no sleep and very little food. I found myself pushing a shopping cart full of junk right past the front door of the most popular gay club in Hollywood, the very place where I had first scored some meth and spent literally every weekend getting loaded ever since. Needless to say, they'd never have to worry about seeing my face in that place again.

When a person gets down to this level of drug addiction, their whole value system has to change. This new crowd that I was meeting both in jail and on the streets was anything but pretentious. Absolutely no one had a job, and absolutely no one that I ever met wanted one. Everybody had some kind of hustle. Some were dealers; others wrote checks; and some broke into houses and cars. Many - both male and female - were prostitutes. I myself was what the street folks called a "booster," elsewhere known as a petty thief or shoplifter. This had always been what I reverted to whenever I needed money.

When it came to boosting, I had always considered myself to be "quite the pro." But one of the primary side effects of using meth – especially in the quantities that I was using – was that it made one extremely paranoid. Imagine walking into a department store and trying to steal something when you're already convinced that everyone around you, including small children and little old ladies, is either a cop or the FBI. And then try to imagine this being your only source of income.

The streets were not a place where I ever chose to be; they were a place were I had to be. Maybe I wasn't as slick as I used to be, and I sure as hell wasn't as cute as I used to be, but I still needed money, and even more important than that, I needed drugs. That was the thing

– dope was more important than money. All money was good for was buying dope. In fact, my chances of getting ripped off were a whole lot greater when I used cash and I soon came to realize that I could just bypass the money thing altogether. So at this point I became the kind of addict that rarely if ever had any actual cash, but always had something to sell or trade. Believe it or not, I think I actually did better with the junk and stolen merchandise than the people spending money.

In the streets, many if not most people picked up a "handle" or street name. If a guy specialized in stolen credit cards, his name would likely be something like "Credit Card Bob," or "MasterCard Mickey." If stealing cars was more up his alley, then it would likely be something like "Tony Toyota" or "Convertible Connie." People had all kinds of strange names. It was just smart to use a handle, because everyone knew that tweakers (people who use meth) are notorious snitches, and cops use snitches like most people use oxygen. It just didn't make sense to let too many people know your real name.

My handle was "Jabber" because my real hustle was my mouth. I seemed to have a gift for making people like me, and after I got you to like me, I could sell you anything.

In this phase of my long season in earthly hell, I became very much the Meth Monster. Every penny I could scratch together went for buying more drugs. If a hamburger cost two dollars, that was $1.50 too much. Everything I ate I either stole, or got from charity workers.

For a while I lived in an abandoned camper that I had stumbled on during my many hours of prowling the alleys in search of something to steal. But in short order I found myself literally living in the streets. I had no place to go, and I didn't care. All I cared about was where I was going to get my next hit.

As for all of that uninhibited sexual freedom that I had signed up for, well, that turned out to be the cruelest joke of all. Who would want to have sex with a homeless bum? Rubbing filthy bodies together in filthy semi-public places was not my idea of a good time – not even in the drugged-out state that I was almost always in. Besides, who had time for sex? Getting and staying high was a full-time, all-consuming occupation.

The only people I knew who still had any real sex life to speak of were the dealers. And that was only because they had the drugs to pay for it. (Of course a nice clean motel room with a bed and running water didn't hurt either.)

There were plenty of both guys and gals who peddled their bodies to the dealers. These were called "bag chasers." If you were a rock star, you had groupies. And if you were a meth dealer, you most certainly had bag chasers.

TaTa, a fifty-something-year-old queen I'd met in county jail, always had a posse of attractive young guys following him around. "Hey, TaTa," I asked one day. "What's your secret?"

He wrapped a rather big muscular arm around my neck. "Child, you're an old black man, don't nobody want you," Tata lovingly said. "What they want is what you got." (Talk about transference - I happened to be twenty-nine years old at the time.) I later found out that TaTa had been dealing crystal meth since long before most of us had even heard of it. And the wisdom he offered me that day was not very far from the truth. In this new reality, it didn't matter if I was twenty-nine or ninety-nine. The only thing that really mattered was the dope, and who had it.

As with virtually all drugs - whether they be prescription, over the counter, or controlled substances - there are possible side effects. The ones associated with crystal are numerous. Two plagued me in particular.

One was my inability to breathe normally. I spent countless hours hacking and coughing, trying desperately to catch my breath. This alienated me from even the people that were right there in the room with me. Over and over again people would try to convince me that this reaction was all in my head and that there was in fact nothing blocking my air passages. But be that as it may, I simply could not breathe normally. I'm not exaggerating when I say that I did this hacking and coughing thing for hours on end.

The second albatross around my neck was this seemingly unquenchable desire to collect junk. We called this "trashing"or"dumpster diving." Now I know that some people who read these words may be thinking, "Well, now this is getting a little silly." But for me to try to describe my many years as a meth addict and never say one thing about dumpster diving would be much more than a little silly. It would mean perpetrating denial and misinformation. I wonder if I had heard more about dumpster diving and less about hot sex, would I have found the idea of using crystal so irresistible.

Well, one thing is certain, I sure as hell didn't sign on for spending hour after hour, and sometimes day after day looking through other people's garbage. This was a strange and uncontrollable phenomenon, and as far as I could tell, it only affected speed freaks. This was also the way that I wasted the next three years of my life.

I have no doubt that it would have gone on that way even longer if Jimmy had not gotten sick.

There is something I want you to understand about Jimmy and me. Even though we had not been together for several years, and we had certainly gone our separate ways, we still very much loved each other. If Jimmy had been capable of monogamy and if I had been capable of getting angry without hitting him, we would probably never have broken up. There had never been anyone after him. So when he got sick, I was devastated. AIDS was getting closer and closer to home. In fact it couldn't get any closer than this; Jimmy was family.

When I showed up at his doorstep after – yet again – being released from jail, he sat me down and told me that he had been very sick. He had full-blown AIDS. We cried together then, Jimmy and I. In all the years that I had known him, we were never as connected as we were in that moment.

I moved in with him that every night.

This was not good news to his family. I'm sure that they saw me as nothing more than a drug-crazed opportunist. But Jimmy and I both understood very clearly why I had moved back in with him. The two of us being together at this time in his life seemed the most natural thing in the world.

There were still problems, of course. At first I was easily able to keep my street life and my home life separate. I figured that as long as I didn't bring any of my drug buddies or associates home with me all would be well. But slowly over the next couple of years, as Jimmy's health deteriorated, I found it harder and harder to leave him at home alone. Since I couldn't get out there in "the life," "the life" found its way into Jimmy's living room. I had turned his apartment into a drug house.

Jimmy deserved so much better from me. There were people there all the time: people making drug deals, people shooting up in the bathroom, people having sex in the kitchen. Jimmy was dying, and here I was carrying on like he wasn't even there.

I thought for years that the next thing that happened was one of the worst experiences either of us had ever endured. But now, in hindsight, I think it much more likely some kind of supernatural intervention.

It happened so quickly.

I was almost never leaving the apartment. There was really no need to - everything we needed came to us. I was high on meth every waking moment. Crystal Meth is speed and sometimes flying around and around in that tiny little apartment got to be too much. On those nights, usually while Jimmy was asleep, I'd go prowling around the basement of the building where we lived. One night I varied slightly from this routine. There was a recently vacated apartment a couple of doors down the hall from us. So I figured, "What the hell? Why not check it out? Maybe the people left something behind." The next thing I knew, the neighbors were banging at the door with their rather huge dog and the building manager in tow. Not fifteen minutes later, the cops showed up. Maybe they would have just let me go with a warning if it were not for the fact that there was already a warrant out for my arrest.

And that's the last time I ever saw Jimmy again. He was just sitting there on the bed, looking so incredibly fragile and confused, as they took me away in handcuffs.

When I made it to court I was hoping beyond hope that the judge would just give me a slap on the wrist for trespassing, and continue my probation. I wanted so desperately to get back to Jimmy's bedside where I belonged. But that was not to be. I had somehow managed to slip and slide around the city and county jail system for years. It seemed like every time I went before a judge I got a slap on the wrist and a threat of prison time if I came back. Well, the time for idle threats and short stays in the county jail had come and gone. This time when I went before the judge, he said, "Three years in the state penitentiary."

Since I had been a thief in one capacity or another off and on since I was a child, prison had always been a very real fear for me. I think that all people who make their living on the wrong side of the law dread the coming of this day. That was the thing: after a while everybody I knew either died, went crazy, or went to prison.

And as if losing Jimmy and being sent upstate for three years wasn't enough, I had just tested positive for HIV.

In 1991, testing positive did not mean the same thing as it does today. I had every reason to believe that I just might not make it out of prison. According to my lab tests, I had been positive for quite some time.

Nevertheless, even more terrifying than the thought of dying in prison was the thought of living there as a gay man. I had seen all of the same movies that you probably have. "If these animals were willing to rape a straight man," I thought, "what in the hell would they do to me?"

When I arrived at San Quentin State Prison you could have cut my fear and anxiety with a knife. Wouldn't you know that I would be sent to a place all the way at the other end of California? Just my luck. The one thing that I was counting on to make my stay there tolerable was the fact that I knew so many people who were already doing time. Well, that was in southern California; San Quentin sat just north of San Francisco, where I didn't know a living soul.

As it turned out, this is one time that being HIV positive actually worked in my favor. Positive inmates were segregated into a huge one hundred-man dormitory. I'm sure that if anybody were paying attention, they would have seen the tension drain from my face when I identified that over half of the people there were gay. Of course there would be many problems and issues to come up over the next two years, but at least my homosexuality wouldn't be one of them.

From what I understand, Jimmy died in a hospice right around the time that I entered the gates of San Quentin. I guess it was better this way; at least he got the care he needed, and was able to pass away with a degree of dignity.

I had been sentenced to three years, but only had to do about twenty months. When they called me for release in February of 1993, I had every intention of returning to Los Angeles and picking up where I had left off. I was actually kind of proud of myself for being able to complete a prison term at San Quentin. Somehow this made me feel more masculine, and definitely more streetwise. I could hardly wait to get back to the old crowd with all of my lies and embellishments about prison life.

But this was not to be.

Inmates being released from a California prison are generally given two hundred dollars "gate money." This is so that you don't hit the streets completely broke and desperate. As I was getting dressed in the release area, I was informed that since I was from LA, I would only be getting one hundred. This was to ensure that I did in fact return to Los Angeles; I could pick the rest up from my parole officer. Well, that may very well have been their intention, and I'll even concede that to a rational person it would probably make sense. But I was not a rational person. I was a drug addict. And as far as I was concerned, twenty months was a long enough time between hits. I was not about to spend every dime I had on a bus ticket back to LA. Right there in that holding cell, while waiting to be released, I hatched another plan. To this very day I've never returned to Los Angeles.

As strange as it may sound, I was not nearly as excited about getting out of prison as I was about getting that needle back in my arm.

Chapter Six: Dope Dealer

When I arrived in San Francisco in February of 1993, I knew right where to go: Polk, Street.

The Polk was the place where people like me gathered. That's not to say that speed freaks, hustlers and assorted other criminals were the *only* people in and around Polk, Street. It is to say, however, that this was the very reason that I showed up there. I needed to be where my people were. This would be my new Hollywood, Boulevard.

Of course what I really needed to do was: 1) to get my butt back to LA on the first thing smoking, and 2) to report to the parole office before they put out a warrant for my arrest. But like so many other times in my story, I opted to do exactly the wrong thing.

That was the thing about me: no one was ever going to accuse me of letting common sense stand in my way. After I got an idea set in my head that was simply the way it was going to be. I gave absolutely no thought to the possible consequences of my irrational decisions. I had felt that way when I arrived in Los Angeles back in

'76, and now – come hell or high water – San Francisco was to be my new home.

This wasn't my first time in the city. When I was a kid I had lived there for three years with my mother, my two sisters, and Billy Jackson. I had also visited a few times since arriving in California, mostly to party over the weekend. And most recently, back when I was trying to work a twelve-step program, I relapsed and went on a three month long drinking spree there. No, I was certainly no stranger to San Francisco.

Still, one thing had changed since the last time I had been in the city: and that one thing was me. I was simply not the same person. Meth had turned my world upside-down. I didn't think the same way; and I didn't value the same things I had only a few short years before. Consequently, I didn't seek out the same people, places or things. My days of drinking and clubbing had long since been over. I was about to experience "the city" in a completely different way.

I had no way of knowing just how different things could be.

Since the time I'd started doing drugs, it had never been about anything but staying high for me. Sure, when I first started up with crystal, I did a little dealing in the restrooms of the clubs. And then there was that period at Jimmy's place right before I went to prison. But even on my best days I rarely made a dime more than I needed to cop (buy more dope) and maybe eat for that day.

And that seemed to be pretty common with speed freaks. Some of the biggest dealers I knew rode around on bicycles and paid for their hotel room by the day. I suppose there must have been people living better than that, but I sure as hell never met them. Why would I? I was a bum. At least that's the way it had been in LA.

Almost immediately after arriving in San Francisco, however, it became apparent that my luck had changed. On some level, virtually everybody who did drugs the way that I did wanted to be a dealer. It just made good practical sense.

Shooting up meth every day was hard, desperate, and oftentimes humiliating work. Every day meant taking another risk. Imagine having to come up with at least a hundred bucks a day just to stay awake. Then imagine actually being afraid to go to sleep – because to go to sleep inevitably meant waking up in somebody's doorway or laundry room, broke, hungry, and too weak to hustle up your next hit. It was a hard life, and I had certainly paid my dues.

By this time I was in my mid-thirties. I had been on a very long run, and I was tired of living like an animal.

Unfortunately, the desire to deal drugs and the ability to actually function well enough to deal drugs were two entirely different things. No matter how hard I tried over the years, I was never quite able to master the art of using and selling dope at the same time. This was not uncommon; meth was a powerful stimulant that often left one spinning around in circles for hours, barricaded in hotel rooms or – God forbid – rummaging through other people's garbage uncontrollably. Every meth dealer that I ever came across was also an addict. Is it no wonder that you never saw meth dealers riding around in Cadillacs and BMWs? It was considered a major accomplishment if you could hang onto a hotel room, keep dope in your pockets, and wheels on that bicycle.

At least that had been my perception up until this point.

I first saw Fast Freddy (not his real name or handle) standing in front of an adult book store on Polk, Street. I knew instantly that he was a dealer because from the very moment that he turned the corner on to Polk – he was surrounded by tweakers (meth addicts). Most dealers would have shunned drawing that much attention to themselves, but this guy seemed to revel in it. There was something very different about the way that this guy operated.

And boy was he fast. In just the few minutes that I observed him that first time he must have made ten to twelve deals, right out there in the open – and then he was gone. The whole thing was over in six or seven minutes.

The second time I saw him, I made my move. I must have had a few dollars on me that first time, but my MO had always been to find out what kind of merchandise the target was into and then go out and steal it for him or her.

But Fast Freddie had other plans. As I said, Fast Freddy moved fast. He took an immediate liking to me, and after our second or third encounter he decided that I should come and work for him. My first lesson under his tutelage was that pedaling merchandise was for losers. I'd always be living from bag to bag as long as I operated that way. My first work assignment was to count his money, and that is how I got hooked on Fast

Freddy. There were literally hundreds and hundreds of dollars in tiny little crumpled up $10, $20, $50 and $100 bills. The dude had them stuffed in every pocket of every piece of clothing he had on. I had never seen so much money at one time in all of my life. At first I thought, "This dude has got to be nuts." After all he'd only known me for all of three days.

But soon I came to realize that this had been a test. Freddy was a pro. There would always be lots of money and dope around, and if I was going to be working with him he had to know that I could be trusted. A few days later, weighing and bagging the dope was added to my job description. Freddy must have known that this would be an even greater challenge for me, but once again I passed with flying colors. And so began my induction into the world of dealing crystal meth – and this time for profit.

Of course, all of the profit went to Freddy, at least in the beginning. But I was studying this dude like my life depended on it. This was the closest I'd ever come to the "big sack" and I wasn't about to blow it. My association with him made adjusting to life in a new city a whole lot easier. Freddy made everything easy for me. Overnight I went from basically knowing no one in San Francisco to being Freddy's right hand. Wherever you saw Freddy, you saw me and even more importantly, whenever you couldn't find Freddy, you could still get what he had through me. While Freddy was around I was about as good and loyal a "company man" as one could hope to find. But when he got busted, I had no problem stepping into his shoes. I can't say that I got all of Fast Freddy's business when he went "up the river", but I can say that I got more than enough. That's just the way things went in the drug business, especially at the street level. People were going in and out of county jail and state prisons literally every day. One day you'd be counting out thousands of dollars on your hotel room floor, and the next day you're bumming phone change in the lock-up. I once asked Freddy why he didn't just give up the streets altogether and sell weight like all the other big shots. His answer was simple: because most of the profit was in the twenty to fifty dollar sale. I guess in the real world what Freddy was talking about would be the difference between selling wholesale and retail. Only in our world selling retail meant going to jail – a lot.

High risk or not, I had eaten in my last food line. The money started pouring in. Not only did I have the customers, some of the best suppliers were actually contacting me. Word spread fast when somebody was on a roll. Suddenly, after thirty-four years of living, I felt like I had "arrived."

I understand that to most of the world a drug dealer is one of the lowest forms of human scum. But to addicts like me, having control of the drugs elevated you to the status of a minor celebrity. Drugs were our lives, and since we all understood that, what was the sense in pretending that having them in abundance wasn't a big deal? It was a very big deal for a guy like me. Finally, I was having things my way.

But of course having things my way came at a price. Over the next nine years I was sent back to prison nine times. The charges were always the same: possession for sale of a controlled substance. The way the system worked in San Francisco, if you got busted with dope while still on parole, nine times out of ten, the charges were dropped and you were sent back to prison on a violation. This was not a bad deal for me since I was already in violation of my parole by not returning to Los Angeles, so what was a couple of extra months? After the second or third time, going to prison meant nothing to me; it was simply the price I paid for having it my way on the streets. What difference did it make anyway? I had gone to jail just as much back when I was digging through other people's garbage for a living.

This new and improved lifestyle came with other baggage as well. Every day meant walking the fine line between paranoia and legitimate fear about personal safety. Dealing drugs at the street level meant dealing with a wide variety of people from a wide variety of backgrounds. I had to pretend to be tough or at least to be "connected" to "some people" that were, in order to survive. In addition to that, you never knew who that dude was that you just made twenty bucks off of. If he got stopped by the cops for any reason, he could easily rat you out and walk on most charges. He could just as easily set you up to be robbed or played in some way. Few people could be trusted. When you did business with pretty much anybody who had the price of a bag, you could never be sure who the rat was. Everybody knew that, and for those who weren't savvy enough to figure it out on their own, the cops were always there to educate and motivate them. Of the nine times I went to prison on drug charges, eight of them were the result of information obtained by a "confidential informant."

In reality, I probably wasn't selling any more dope than the guys riding around on bicycles. But in my mind

I was big – so big in fact that I never once owned a car, had an apartment, or even my own furniture. What was the point? I was always on my way back to prison anyway.

The way it worked out, my time inside and my freedom were divided in three equal parts: one third of my time was spent on the streets of San Francisco, and the other two thirds belonged to the state of California. Of course these were just averages; there were a few times when I was only on the streets a couple of weeks.

I guess in a twisted sort of way it did make sense that I would never acquire anything of any real value. I was first and foremost a drug addict; there was nothing on this planet that I valued more than dope. The more money I made the more meth I bought.

If there was ever one thing that virtually all small time drug dealers had in common, it was a propensity to brag about how much dope they got busted with. Many would walk around in jail showing their arrest report just to prove it; many others would simply lie. It was a strange and shallow value system, but for people like me, it was simply reality. Drugs meant everything, and the more drugs you had, the more valuable a person you were… period.

The next really stupid thing I did in San Francisco was to get emotionally involved with a straight man. I know this sounds a little strange; how could this dude possibly be straight if he was involved with me? But in the underworld of meth users, the lines between sexual orientations got very blurry. You see, it really was all about the drugs for a lot of people. I knew countless numbers of heterosexual men who had sex with men on a regular basis and still considered themselves straight. A few years earlier I would have said that this was bull, that any man who had sex with other men, had to be at least bisexual. But that was only because I hadn't lived long enough yet. Hustlers did it, many men in prison did it, and down-and-out drug addicts definitely did it. Not everybody, but definitely lots. That's not to say that all of these guys were just in it for the money or the drugs. I also encountered many men who I strongly suspect were doing crystal meth specifically for the purpose of having sex with men. Let me put it like this: if I were straight and yet every time I shot up crystal I found myself in bed with a man, and then I continued to shoot up crystal a on regular basis, what would that make me? After all, there were many other drugs out there if all I wanted to do was get high, right?

To this day I'm not really sure where my friend (let's call him Cory) fit into this blurriness, but whatever it was that went on between us, it went on for eight years. When I first met Cory he was standing on a dimly lit corner on Polk, Street. No big mystery there; to anyone who might have been watching, he was obviously a hustler and I was just as obviously trying to pick him up. To my amazement he actually turned me down the first time. Not that I thought that I was some kind of irresistible catch or anything. But he was working as a prostitute at the time. Things had been going very well for me in the drug business, and frankly I just wasn't used to being turned down – especially not by hustlers. Naturally I thought it was because he was a racist, but a few weeks later when I asked him why he wouldn't go with me the first time, he took a chance and told me the truth. "I didn't go with you, Jabber," he said, "because you didn't have any teeth and because I just didn't think you had any money." "Out of the mouths of babes." Oh well, I couldn't very well fault him there. What he said was the exact truth, or I should say, half of the exact truth. I had just had all of my top teeth pulled at San Quentin, and was then paroled before the dentures were ready. The funny thing was not one other person had made mention of this since I arrived in San Francisco, and I had almost forgotten that I had no front grill. This was another benefit of using meth, no less than a third of the people I knew were missing all or most of their teeth. Anyway, I liked this dude right off the top.

I was thirty-six at this time and Cory was twenty-four and man oh man, what a great looking dude this was. To me he was the character played by Brad Pitt in the movie, "Thelma and Louise." Even though he never told me this, I'm sure that someone on the street must have told him who I was and what I did for a living, because the second time I approached him there was no hesitation. In fact, the second time Cory approached me. So sure, we both knew where we stood from the beginning – except wasn't he supposed to ask me for money, or drugs, or something?

Cory and I became quick friends and we hung out together a lot, but it wasn't until we wound up in jail together that things were taken to another level. It was not the custom in the San Francisco county jail system to put black and white men together in the same cell. But for some reason we were able to slip through the cracks and it was there in that cell that we became emotionally involved. I choose not to use the phrase "fell in love" only because that would imply that we were both equally invested. In hindsight I can see that I was probably to Cory what Fast Freddy had been to me. I knew and played the drug game well, and Cory wanted in. That's not to say that we weren't close. During the couple of mouths we spent locked in that cell together, Cory and I became about as close as I had been with anybody since I lost Jimmy. What complicated matters was the fact that he wasn't really gay, and I certainly was. Someone was obviously going to get hurt, and since it wasn't Cory...

But for the moment things were going well.

We both went on to prison from there – me on another violation, and Cory for the first time. A few months later, when we got out around the same time, we hooked up as partners (in crime).

Freddy's first important advice to me had been that I should give up boosting and get serious about making money. Now I was telling Cory that he'd never make a dime until he gave up crack. (When I met him he was addicted to both crystal meth and crack cocaine. Both were bad, but crack was worse, at least on the wallet.) To my amazement he gave it up, just like that. In no time flat, Cory was making his own money. But he didn't take off – as many thought he would as soon as he was able. Instead he invited me to his wedding! I couldn't believe it. Just as casually as if he were telling me that he wore a size 10 ½ tennis shoe, Cory informed me that he was engaged to be married. That's what I mean about him not being gay; I think that even a bisexual man would have had the sensitivity to realize that I would be devastated over this. To me our relationship meant everything; to him it obviously meant nothing.

Well, no matter how I felt about it, Cory got married. And then about seven months later he became a father. Then five months after that he was separated, and shortly after that Cory was divorced. The whole thing from beginning to end lasted about two years. And yes I was still hanging around on the sidelines for all of those two years. Not that I was wanting or waiting for him and his wife to break up. They had produced a beautiful baby boy, and I was actually hoping that they could make it work. Be that as it may, in short order Cory was back in the life. However, things would never be the same between us, no matter how desperately I wanted them to be.

Meanwhile, there were other interesting developments.

I can remember very clearly what I was doing the day that I heard about a revolutionary new class of HIV medications. Apparently people were going from near death to relatively good health and in a relatively short time. Actually it's very easy to remember what I was doing and where I was doing it, because at the time I was at what had become my primary residence – a locked cell at San Quentin State Prison. That's where I was, and what I was doing is even easier: absolutely nothing. That's what you did an awful lot of during the time while you were in the reception center waiting to be housed. It was either read a book, or write a letter, or do nothing.

At any rate, this was very good news for a guy who had been diagnosed with full-blown AIDS (based on my t-cell count) three years earlier. It was indeed good news, but it wasn't enough to make me give up dope. By the time I came back a year later the new drugs (protease inhibitors) were available to inmates, but the prison doctor refused to put me on them. He and I both knew the way that I lived on the streets. Careless and inconsistent use of these drugs would render them ineffective forever, and there was no turning back after you became resistant. At the time I was very angry, but now I can see that this prison doctor may very well have saved my life.

This would have been a very good time to get off of drugs. After all, the pharmaceutical companies had managed to package hope in a capsule – now all I had to do was cooperate. Fear and hopelessness had played a major part in why there had been virtually no serious attempts at trying to get clean since I left AA and NA several years earlier.

Granted, you didn't have to have a terminal illness to become a dope fiend. But if you did happen to have a terminal illness and you were already a dope fiend, what would be your motivation to stop? I for one was not the least interested in putting the kind of work it took into getting clean and sober only to watch myself slowly waste away and eventually die. The way I saw it, as long as I stayed high and chemically kept reality at bay, I wouldn't have to think about such things. But of course it was inevitable that reality would have its day.

I realize that this may sound a little strange, but at least in regards to my health, all of this time that I was spending behind bars was actually working in my favor. The state was inadvertently saving me from my self-destructive self and extending my life expectancy. I knew plenty of people who were HIV-positive, shot up crystal meth daily and never went to jail or prison. Unfortunately, every time I got released most of these guys were a little further along in the progression of the disease. And I'm sorry to say that many of those guys who somehow managed to never get in trouble with the law are no longer with us. Those of us who seemed to be doing life "on the installment plan" were faring a little better, if for no other reason than we were actually only getting high on the average three or four months a year. Even though the doctors refused to put me on the very potent protease inhibitors, I was still leaving prison relatively healthy every few months.

Obviously this couldn't and wouldn't go on forever. Back on the streets, things were slowly beginning to change within my body. Even though I was still shooting up crystal three or four times a day, it was getting harder and harder to get out there and ply my trade. Drug dealing could be both physically and mentally exhausting. Physically, because you absolutely had to keep moving. Drug addicts were notoriously disloyal. The only way to stay ahead of the game was to keep yourself perpetually available; nobody was going to hold on to the money for you. And mentally, because it seemed like virtually everybody was trying to get over. If you let your defenses down even for a moment, you could find yourself counting fake money at the end of the night.

It wasn't that I was sick exactly. More like I was getting progressively weaker. To anyone who happened to be observing, I'm sure that I had much more of the appearance of someone on heroin than speed. To make matters worse, I made the mistake of accepting large quantities of meth up front (before paying for it.) This was a very bad decision; now I absolutely had to produce. I needed to come up with a thousand dollars a day just to break even. What complicated matters even more was that after I hooked up with these guys, quality control went right out the window. Since I perpetually owed them money, I had to take whatever they gave me. Good drugs sold themselves; third rate crap took a lot more work. I was exhausted.

But the real beginning of the end came for me when I got robbed. I wish I could remember where I first heard the saying, "To call some people, God could use a feather; for others it takes a brick."

Chapter Seven: Coming Out

In the year 2000, I encountered something I finally recognized as evil.

All my life I had lived with a deeply rooted fear of any kind of physical violence. I have no doubt that this fear was inextricably tied to the extreme domestic violence I witnessed as a small child. I never learned to fight, and had zero interest in exerting physical dominance over any living thing. Violence had been the catalyst for abruptly ending both of my significant relationships. And now, in the year 2000, it became once again the catalyst for change.

I don't believe for a second that God assigned a man to come out from between two parked cars and smash a beer bottle over my head. But because I know that he has such an intricate knowledge of me, I believe that he allowed it to happen. My Lord knew exactly what it would take to bring me out. In all of the years that I had used and sold drugs, never once had I come face to face with this, my greatest fear. I had spent half a lifetime surviving by my wits alone, but now there was no opportunity for talking my way out of this situation. My reaction was swift – I ran screaming into oncoming traffic.

No doubt this was the beginning of the end of my drug addiction and life of crime. But make no mistake – it was just that, the *beginning* of the end.

This business of running away when I was attacked had the potential of becoming a very serious problem for me. Word spread fast when a dealer got hit. As a rule you couldn't be both a coward and a drug dealer at the same time. Once you got tagged as an easy mark, the vultures would start circling. The only way to save face would be to retaliate swift and hard.

But who was I kidding? I was the kind of guy who hesitated before stepping on a cockroach.

Besides that, I still had other pressing issues to deal with, especially with my new connection. The harder I worked, it seemed, the deeper I got into debt. Back in the early days, when I first arrived in San Francisco, I could have turned this situation around with my eyes closed. But by this time I had been living with full-blown AIDS (as defined by my T-cell counts) for six or seven years. Truth told all I really wanted to do was find a nice soft bed somewhere and lie down. But of course I couldn't do that – not as long as I was in debt and holding someone else's merchandise.

This would have been a very good time to go to jail. If you got busted, and kept your mouth shut, all drug debts would be cancelled. This would also give this whole situation with the attempted robbery a chance to cool off – I wouldn't be expected to retaliate if I were locked up. And of course the other benefit would be that I could finally get some much-needed rest.

As if spiritual forces were looking out for me, that is exactly what happened. Not two weeks after the beer-bottle-man struck, the cops were once again at my door.

Although this was my third time to be sent to CMC (California Men's Colony) in San Luis Obispo, right from the beginning I could tell that this time was going to be very different. The first evidence of change was in my attitude, specifically toward the streets, doing time, and drugs in general. It was as if suddenly a veil had been lifted from my eyes, and now I could finally see my life for what it was. Gone were my usual stories, my bragging, and my embellishments of my exploits on the mean streets of San Francisco.

Gone also was the desire to return to them.

The Bible says that no man cometh unto God unless he be drawn. Well, there's no question that I was being drawn or pulled by "something."

The next significant change came when I, Timothy Blaine, showed up at the doors of the prison chapel. Understand that although I had identified that I wanted to turn my life around; this was not the logical next step for me. As a young man, I had been schooled in the ways of the twelve steps of Alcoholics Anonymous. In my mind, recovery from drugs and alcohol was synonymous with working a twelve-step program. Still, there was something much deeper pulling at me. Could it be this business of mortality – that my tired and worn-out body and soul were telling me to prepare myself for the inevitable? I don't know what it was, but there was something deep within me telling me that I needed something more than to simply get off drugs. The drugs were only a symptom of the spiritual emptiness and despair that went all the way to the core of my being.

So here I was after all of these years, attending a Christian church of my own volition. I hadn't been inside a chapel since my sister's wedding back in 1977, and before that my attendance was at best sporadic, mostly on holidays or for the occasional wedding.

It's not that I hadn't been exposed to church early on. Like in many African-American families, my grandmother had tried her best to keep us all grounded there. But in my youth, my mother just was not very interested in going to church, so for the most part my immediate family didn't go. Ironically, now, in the year 2000, my mother was the very person witnessing to me – in fact, this had been going on for several years.

At first I thought my mom had gone a little soft in the head. I'd write her long letters from prison trying to explain my circumstances and maybe talk about current events, and she'd fire back with five or six pages of Scripture. I'd ask her how my sisters and their families were doing, and she'd answer with quotes from Romans or Galatians. If I asked how the weather was, I'd likely get, "John, Luke, and Mathew." At the time I simply wasn't ready to receive the message she was trying so desperately to convey, and many of those letters were merely scanned over and thrown to the back of my locker. But now, in my hour of need, I had to concede that my mother had undergone a profound and dramatic change. Never had I known her to be so passionate about anything. I had certainly seen it in my grandmother, and I knew how seriously the world in general took various religions. But after all, this was my own mother, the one person that I had known since the day of my birth and before. She was simply not the kind of woman to be easily converted to faith in anything. Nor was she likely to join a church or any other institution or organization merely for community, or a sense of belonging. Most plainly put, my mother was anything but a "people person." No, whatever had happened to my mom, she certainly wasn't faking it; she was without a doubt Christian.

Now I had to wonder, was it possible that there might be something locked away in that ancient text for me as well? With all of my negative history and my unbridled capacity for self-delusion and self-destruction, any change would have to be profound and radical. So what about this Jesus – who was he really? How did this whole thing work? Had the time come for me to find out?

Dare I open that Bible?

I'll be the first to admit that up until this point I had done virtually no investigation into the Christian experience. But even with my limited knowledge, I had long thought that there was something very suspicious about this perception that God was only the God of people who got married and had babies.

There's no question that my process had begun by this time, but it wasn't going to be like on television. I didn't just walk through the doors of the prison chapel and then thirty minutes later lay my burdens – including over twenty years of drug addiction – down on the altar. (That's not to say that I don't believe that God can and sometimes will do that, it's only to say that that is not my testimony.) Still, I did feel like I was through with drugs, and I went about making plans like a person who was not returning to "the life."

The first thing I had to do was to try to get my parole officially switched from Los Angeles to San Francisco. By this time I had been living in San Francisco illegally for seven or eight years and I saw no reason to return to LA. Jimmy was dead, and all of my most recent memories of my life there were not good. However, if I was serious about not returning to prison (and I believe that I was), I could no longer do things my way. Being in the wrong city was most definitely a guaranteed ticket back. No, whether I chose to stay clean or not, until I got off parole, my butt still belonged to the State of California. This time I had to play by their rules. Right up until the day I was scheduled to parole, all I could get anyone to say in regards to my transfer was "we're working on it." The system was not very enthusiastic about transferring inmates from city to city. After all, why should San Francisco want to take on LA's problems? They already had more than their share of convicted drug dealers on the street.

But there was a possible loophole. If I could find a drug program in San Francisco that was willing to take me, the parole department might approve the transfer.

So this became the next short-term goal: I needed to find a program. A large percentage of the people in prison were in for some kind of drug-related offense, either directly or indirectly. Sure, a lot of these men did their crimes for money, but an awful lot of that money was used to buy drugs. Consequently, there was a wealth of information available to the asking on the various drug programs up and down the West Coast. When I narrowed the search down to the Bay Area, one name kept coming up: Walden House. Of course the down side of that was that all of the former clients I was talking to were obviously back in prison. But that was no indication of how many didn't come back. Besides, I had to start somewhere. I set my sights on Walden House.

First, through the mail, I pleaded my case to Walden. And then I began the tedious process of trying to convince the powers that be to take me seriously and allow me to go there. Of course everyone in prison had a story of redemption, and I'm sure that the counselors and the parole department had heard it all hundreds if not thousands of times before. Fortunately, there were outside agencies that would advocate and assist those inmates who wanted to go into rehab upon their release.

My stumbling block was this issue of returning to San Francisco – as far as the state (prison system) was concerned I was still a resident of Los Angeles. When I was called to the counselor's office and informed that the San Francisco police department had placed a hold on my release and would be picking me up at the gate, I should have been angry, instead I thought, "Well, perhaps this will work in my favor. At least I'll be back in the city."

When my parole date rolled around, sure enough, transporters from the City and County of San Francisco were at the prison waiting to pick me up. The warrant was a small matter, but I'd have to stay in jail at least long enough to see a judge.

When I was finally released to the streets three weeks later, Walden informed me that there was nothing they could do for me, and that I should call my parole agent in Los Angeles immediately. I hung up the phone, and I don't think it was a full forty-five minutes before I had a needle in my arm – that's about how long it took to walk to Polk, Street. Just like that. Every sane and sensible thought I had been having over the last eight or nine months went right out the window.

Moreover, it really is true that addicts only have control over the first hit. After that, if anyone had dared bring up the idea of going into a drug program, I would have either politely or impolitely suggested they get the hell out of my face.

So here I was on yet another drug run, and yet again running on parole. Of course not much had changed on the streets. But "the game," as I knew it, would never be the same.

For one thing, I understood my body somewhat better. Just as soon as I started running around like a lunatic chasing every dollar, eating once a day, and sleeping twice a week, I was going to start feeling like I had AIDS all over again. And for what? The cops always ended up with the money, the drugs got destroyed, and I'd go right back to where I came from – prison. No, my money-chasing days were over. But because I took that first hit, my addiction was alive and well.

Of course getting high still took cash, so I didn't get completely out of the drug business. In fact I was back in business within a few minutes after I did that first hit; at this point there was no way for me to separate the two. I was not about to go back to shoplifting, and to be honest I still very much enjoyed the status and constant validation I got as a meth dealer. Besides, at forty two, I was a little "long in the tooth" to be sleeping in the streets.

However, at this point my primary concern was avoiding apprehension. Since moving back to Los Angeles was out of the question, I would always be a fugitive. This had been the case since the day I arrived in San Francisco eight or nine years earlier, but somehow now I became much more aware of the insanity of walking around delivering drugs door-to-door. So everything got scaled down. I rarely left my hotel room, and only did business with a few people that I "thought" I knew well.

In reality, of course, I didn't know any of those people who I sold drugs to. So what happened, and in relatively short order, was what always happened – I got set up and I found myself back behind bars.

This time they didn't send me right back to prison. That small matter for which I was extradited back to SF for a few months earlier had become a big matter when I didn't show up for the second court date. Somehow I had managed to be on both parole and probation at the same time. It was a complicated situation, but the judge came up with a way to make it uncomplicated: "Three years in the State penitentiary."

"Be careful what you wish for," as they say in A.A. Or is it "Be careful what you pray for"? Well, I don't think I was praying just yet, but I do know that I very much wanted this issue with the parole department to go away. The situation seemed hopeless – and then, just like that, it was gone. With one rap of the judge's gavel I became a legal resident of the City and County of San Francisco – at least in the eyes of the penal system. Since the latest crime and conviction took place in SF, that's where I'd be living, at least for the first three years after my release. As it turned out, the three-year sentence wasn't even going to be as bad as I originally thought. I had somehow accumulated a lot of credit for time served and wasn't actually going to be doing much more than the usual seven or eight months that I always did. Things seemed to be moving slowly in my favor.

And then all hell broke loose, this time in my body.

In the ten years or so since I had been diagnosed with HIV, I had yet to experience any real illness – mostly just a general kind of weakness and soreness in my legs. But all of that was about to change. While waiting for yet another court date (a formality involving sentencing), I woke up in the middle of the night, soaking wet, shivering violently, and with diarrhea so persistent that I felt like every drop of fluid was being violently pushed from my body. Never before had I felt so deathly ill or so powerless.

But the things that were going on within my body were by no means the worst part of this experience. No, the very worst part was being heckled by other inmates as I desperately tried to make it the two or three steps from my bunk to the toilet. I had to do this over and over and over until finally I heard someone yell, "Hey cop! I think that faggot with AIDS is dying in there!"

This was not a call for help out of any concern for me or for what I might be going through. As, one of the other hecklers so colorfully put it, "Get dat stankin' motha fucka outa here!"

And I prayed. "Dear God, please, not like this. Please don't let me die in a place like this." The next thing I knew, I was being rushed by ambulance to the jail ward of the county hospital, where the doctors gave me a prescription for Imodium and sent me back to jail. But the next night, I was back again, and with a temperature of 105 degrees.

While I lay in that hospital bed, not knowing what was wrong with me or how long I'd be there, Cory decided to show his true colors. Yes, Cory was still very much in the picture at this time. At the very least I thought of him as my best friend. But in truth, I had never really gotten over him and I still held on to the idea that what we had was more than a mere friendship. I must have called the place where he had been staying fifteen or twenty times before one of the roommates there took pity on me and told me what was going on.

When you sell drugs at the street level, you can hardly help but accumulate a lot of (mostly stolen) property. This was especially true with me, I think, because I had spent so much time on the other end, selling everything I could get my hands on for the next hit. All of this "stuff" usually disappeared when I got busted anyway, but since Cory and I both happened to be on the streets at the same time I thought nothing of having him pick my keys up at the jail. The idea was that he would pack up my belongings and put them in a storage unit that I kept. Instead he packed up my belongings and sold them. After that, he proceeded to the aforementioned storage unit and cleaned it out as well.

I don't think that this betrayal was a big part of my "bottom" and subsequent coming out of "the life." Instead it was yet another piece of my former self being chipped away. It felt sort of like being kicked in the stomach while you were already on the ground.

When I arrived at San Quentin several weeks later I was still very sick, but even more determined than ever to turn what was left of my life around. The incident with the beer-bottle-man had certainly woken me up. Relapsing only moments after things didn't go my way told me that this was not going to be an easy journey to recovery. Cory's betrayal only magnified how truly alone in the world I was.

But how can I make you understand? It was when I got sick – this was the thing that sent me running into the arms of Jesus.

As I often tell my friends, I first became interested in Jesus Christ because I thought that I might be meeting him very soon. My perspective on sickness and death was not like other people in their early forties. I had seen far too much death already, and now in this prolonged illness I was very afraid. Life and the possibilities of what lies after death became very real, very serious concerns. Even though I was not "churched" and had very little knowledge of Scripture, as far as I knew there was only one name given under heaven by which I could be saved. I didn't even know what "being saved" meant exactly – I only knew that if God had made a provision for mankind by which he wouldn't burn in hell forever, I didn't want to miss it for lack of knowledge.

For about a year at this point, I had been feeling like I was being somehow handled by God or supernatural forces.

Now I had to wonder: was the reason for this something much bigger than my drug addiction? Was the Lord calling me home *now*? Is that what this was all about – was I really going to die soon? The symptoms of my illness were slowly going away, but the spiritual call on my life would not diminish. Why was this thing happening to me? Half the people I knew had AIDS, yet they didn't all go running to Jesus at the first sign of trouble.

Or did they? How would I know? People tended to disappear when they got sick. Granted I knew an awful lot of people who had passed away, but I certainly hadn't been at any of their bedsides at the end. I had never "been there" for anybody but myself. The way I had carried on at Jimmy's apartment at the end of his life had been a disgrace. Besides, who'd be talking about their spiritual condition with their drug dealer anyway? "As far as I know," I thought, "this thing going on inside of me might be as natural as rain watering trees."

This time I was sent to a medical facility which also happened to be a prison in Vacaville, California. Right away I started attending Sunday morning services and taking tracts back to my cell afterwards. Frankly, I was having a very hard time with the Bible. I was overwhelmed with the thousands of little tiny words. Beginning at the beginning was simply not working for me – I was far too hungry and far too anxious to burrow though hundreds and hundreds of pages of the history of God and the world. Everything seemed so distant and irrelevant to the world I lived in today. I became very frustrated, but not totally discouraged. You see, I had to know this God. With every passing day I felt more and more as though He were somehow calling me.

There was a small group of inmates that met regularly for Bible study in the common area of the unit where I lived. This group was led by what most folks would call a "jail house preacher." Say or think what you will about people who find the Lord after being locked away for an extended amount of time, but I have yet to find a man with any stronger faith. There was a very good chance that this man would never see another day of physical freedom on Earth, but to look into his eyes, you could never tell it. This lifer was already free. I admired him and the way he was doing his time, at first from afar.

I think it both strange and profoundly sad that I felt like this man who was so well versed in Scripture would not minister to me because I was gay. "So you're gay and I'm a murderer," he said when I told him of this apprehension. "Now let's talk about the gospel of Jesus Christ."

I learned a lot from this brother in the months to come, but there was one thing that I got from him that would profoundly influence the course of my spiritual walk, as well as the issues associated with my health, my addiction and all other areas of my life. I approached him about my frustration over this issue I was having with reading the Bible for myself. I told him that I had never read a full page of the Bible in my entire life. I told him that the only books that could hold my interest were real-life crime stories. I told him about what a lousy student I'd been, and about how I'd never learned to study. I even told him about my stifling fear of what I had always heard was written there about me or people "like me."

To all of this he said, "Jabber, I want you to do this: when they call 'lock up,' I want you to go back to your cell and pray. Ask God to remove whatever is standing in the way of you reading his word. Ask it in the name of Jesus Christ." "And then I would begin in the New Testament."

When I got back to my cell I did just that. And then I opened my eyes, picked up the Bible and I began to read. And read, and read, and read. Just like that, I began my journey into what I had always heard was the word of God.

This was no small matter – suddenly God became much more than just a decision to believe in Him, so much more also than an intellectual concept of who He is. On that day, in that cell, on that hard prison bunk, God became real to me. And not only was He real, but I, Timothy Blaine, could actually talk to Him. To think that God had just heard and answered my prayer before I could even open my eyes was overwhelming to say the least. What kind of power had I just tapped into? I had to know more.

Where as up to this point I hadn't been able to read and comprehend even one page of the Bible, now I couldn't seem to put it down. Every day I'd rush back to my cell, I wanted so desperately to know every word that came out of the mouth of Jesus Christ. Memorizing key passages and the names and authors of all the books in the New Testament became self-imposed homework assignments. I wanted to know who had answered my prayer – was it God, Jesus, the Spirit living inside of me?

I remember being especially curious about the apostle Paul. Who was he exactly, and why had his letters become Scripture? Questions, questions, questions – each night I'd study and then just as soon as the gates popped open I'd ambush the preacher man with more questions. Never in my life had I been so excited about anything, or so hungry for knowledge. In all honesty, in the beginning I did not want to leave the four Gospels, and that's exactly where I stayed. In the life of Christ I found hope such as I never dreamed I could experience. Over and over, backwards and forwards, I studied these four accounts of the life of Jesus Christ as if my very life depended on it. I felt that way back then, and that's largely the way I feel even today.

But because Jesus Himself continually referred to and quoted the written Scriptures, I had to dig deeper.

Because of the spiritual way that I view life today, I find it harder and harder to accept the concept of pure coincidence. As I look back over the events that gradually brought me from the person I had been to the person I am today, I can plainly see that there was no coincidence at all. This was a spiritual calling, and even though I didn't have a clue as to what that meant, I was beginning to trust the one doing the calling more than I trusted myself.

Right around this same time, my mother decided that she "had had enough, and she wasn't going to take it any more."

At the time I thought, "Well now, this has got to be about the strangest thing since French fried ice cream." Here this woman had been diligently trying to both witness and minister to me for some six or seven years, and now when at long last I was finally ready to talk about Jesus, she decides to cut all communication with me.

Of course many – if not most – parents of drug addicts and habitual criminals come to this same place at some point in their relationship with their self-destructive offspring. But I thought the timing of this particular separation especially strange. And that was just the point – it had all been strange.

Just a little over a year prior to this, I had been a carefree dope fiend, peddling my particular brand of poison around the Tenderloin district of San Francisco, oblivious to the workings of either God or the devil. Now I was sure that God was separating me from everyone and everything that I knew, or thought that I knew. I believe that the Lord was teaching me that the only one whom I could or should depend on was Him.

There is a popular motto used in both the prison system and in recovery programs: "If you fail to plan, you plan to fail." So I went about making my exit plan for the second time in a year. This time things would be considerably easier – for one thing, this time I'd be paroling to San Francisco. The next step was getting into a residential treatment facility. Since I was already familiar with Walden House, I gave them another call.

This time they told me that since I was now a legal resident they could pretty much guarantee that I'd get in. There was still one obstacle, however, and that obstacle was me.

After the way that whole scenario had played out the last time I got released, I was not at all confident that I could make it from Vacaville all the way back to the city, and then into the program by myself. A drug call could come in a blinding and powerful surge of energy, especially for a person who's been locked up for awhile. I couldn't afford to leave anything to chance. So the next part of my plan was to find an outside agency that would be willing to pick me up at the gate and physically deliver me into the hands of Walden House. This was both a lesson in humility and a reality-check for me – it meant accepting who and what I was at this particular time in my life. It also meant learning to ask for help.

I was talking to God a lot by this time, and I often felt His presence near me, but at the same time I was beginning to look at things in a practical no-nonsense kind of way. Maybe this was the way He was answering my prayers; maybe God was teaching me how to think and make rational decisions for myself based on the facts that were available to me. Maybe God was teaching me to be honest.

It is with a degree of shame and embarrassment that I must admit something about this juncture in my life: I was actually afraid to leave prison.

Chapter Eight: Program

This time everything went smoothly, and in the year 2001, I began my adventure into rehab. Walden House would prove to be the right choice at the right time. Not only was I a hardcore meth addict, but I was also an ex-convict who up until this time had made his living either by stealing or selling dope. I hadn't held a job or participated in society in any significant way in over sixteen years. To me, Walden seemed to be the "one-stop shop" for recovery in the Bay Area. Even though the name suggested that it was some kind of a house that I was being released to, they had grown to much more than that since the 1960s. This was now Walden House – the corporation.

They even had a special facility for people living with and learning to cope with HIV. This component was especially useful to me since I didn't really know very much about this disease I had been living with for many years now. In the past, too much talk about AIDS or sickness made me very uncomfortable. But now, if I was going to do battle with this thing, I wanted to know exactly what I was up against. Lesson number one: I was not necessarily dying, but an awful lot of that was going to depend on me. A lot had changed since I had stopped paying attention.

A couple of months later I was moved to one of their big facilities. When I walked through the doors of "the big house," the very first thing I noticed was several people sitting in chairs in isolated areas around the lobby, eyes staring at the floor. "Now wait a minute," I thought. "I couldn't even do that as a child." I can't recall how many times I had been suspended from school because I refused to take their paddling or other humiliating disciplinary actions. If the powers-that-be pushed the issue, I'd simply cuss them out, therefore guaranteeing my suspension. If at forty two I was going to be asked to go and sit in the corner, I smelled trouble on the horizon.

While I was still processing these thoughts, I was informed that the empty chair by the door was for me, and that I was to bow my head and keep my eyes on the floor. The only other option was to use the door.

There were many rules at Walden, and many possible disciplinary actions that could be taken if those rules were not followed – not the least of which was being thrown (though not literally) out on your butt. But to my amazement I seemed to be sailing straight through. No "write-ups," no run-ins with either the staff or the other clients, and most importantly, absolutely no desire to get high. The parole department was pleased, my family was overjoyed, and for all intents and purposes things seemed to be going very well for me at last.

And then I got my first "pass."

I remember very clearly leaving the house that afternoon with absolutely no thought or desire to use. This was my very first time out on a pass alone. Up until this time, every time I'd left the house I was with a "buddy" or in a group. The idea was to gradually reintegrate you back into society. First you simply never left the house, and then never by yourself, and then you'd get a four-hour pass to leave the house alone on the weekend. I don't recall exactly what was supposed to happen after that, because that's as far as I made it.

As I said, there were many rules in program. One of them was that clients couldn't attend parades, street fairs or other public celebrations where there were likely to be people using drugs or alcohol. Some of the rules made little sense to me, but the reason for this particular one was obvious enough. If I had only had the presence of mind to look back into my own personal history, I would have realized that my relapse and subsequent downward spiral into serious drug addiction was ignited at the Gay Pride parade back in LA over seventeen years earlier.

But now, in the year 2001, my devious and drug-abused mind chose to completely block that memory. On the surface, though, it all started innocently enough.

San Francisco has many such (off-limits for us) fairs, parades and celebrations during the summer months, and at least five of these are specifically gay. As in most big cities, Pride (the gay pride parade) is the biggest, and in SF the Folsom Street Fair is number two. I wanted very much to go to this event, but I was not willing to break the rules and draw negative attention to myself over it. So after I asked for permission and was refused, I let the whole thing go. Or so I thought. To make a long story short, I switched days with someone and went out on my pass on the same day as the fair. I think it's important to note that I was not consciously planning on getting high or even on attending the fair. Yet in hindsight I can see that my actions were organized and deliberate. When I got off the bus in the Castro (SF's gayest neighborhood), there was a very attractive, scantily dressed man coming towards me. As we passed, he smiled and then stopped and asked me for directions to the fair. And that was all it took.

Just like that, I forgot all about the program, sobriety, God and anything and everything else that stood in the way of me getting that needle back in my arm. Of all the things that I have experienced in life, this one thing remains the most baffling. What was I thinking in that moment? And what about the moments before and after that? I can remember very clearly walking the two or three miles to the fair because I was too anxious to wait for a bus. And I also recall desperately needing to use the restroom on my way, but being unwilling to break my pace even for that.

When I finally got to the big fair, I might as well have been at the beach or at home in bed for that matter. This thing was not about any fair – I don't even like fairs. From the beginning, this whole thing had been about getting high. But even then I did not consciously know that.

I know that people get a little uncomfortable when someone starts talking about demons, devils and evil spirits. And I'll be the first to admit that I know little to nothing about the spiritual realm or who and what lives in it.

But I do know this: there is an enemy. I don't know if he lives in my head, my heart, or slithers from beneath the ground. I only know that he does exist, and he does have *some* power. I have come to believe that just as surely as there is a Holy God who wants good in the earth and in me personally, there is simultaneously something dark and evil that wants nothing more than to keep me separated from Him.

The enemy is real, and he wasn't through with me yet.

And so, I marched on through this Folsom Street Fair, desperately looking for a familiar face, oblivious to everything around me. The only thing that mattered at this point was finding that one set of eyes that would give me drugs. I was only allowed to leave Walden with ten bucks in my pocket, so I couldn't just walk up to a stranger.

This was a clever demon that I was dealing with; he knew to first separate me from the pack, and to then attack. The Folsom Street Fair had served its purpose.

What a devious trick this whole thing had been. The kind of dope fiends I knew didn't hang out in street fairs or any other public places for that matter. No, my old crowd hibernated during the day, and then prowled the streets in the dark hours. So I abandoned the Fair and found my way back to the Tenderloin – and within a few minutes I was back at the mercy of the devil. You see, that was all it took to recapture this slave. It all came down to that first hit. After the drug reentered my body, I went right back to being Jabber, the dope fiend.

What a hopeless and pitiful feeling it was coming down from that first high and wondering what the hell had happened. It was like I had been in some kind of trance from the moment I passed that guy on the street in the Castro to the time I finally got that loaded syringe back in my arm.

"And when exactly did this whole thing really begin anyway?" I asked myself. Surely it was before passing some stranger on the street. What was this obsession with going to a street fair that I had never gone to even when I was using? There were many such questions to ask myself, but I chose to deal with the situation in the same way that virtually all practicing drug addicts deal with hard questions: I got high again, and again, and again.

But whereas I'd usually just keep going and going and going until the cops showed up and took me back to prison, this time I got lucky. This time I went to the emergency room.

Acute dehydration – coupled with an overdose of another drug called GHB – was the diagnosis in the ER. I had managed to drop forty pounds in about three weeks. In the old days I could easily have bounced back from this episode with a few days of rest and fluids, but this wasn't the old days. I was a very sick man when I finally picked up that phone. Fortunately, Walden did take me back, although not at the same facility. This time I was to try the program in a much smaller and more intimate setting. The parole department decided to give me a one-time pass as well, since I did somehow make it back to the safety zone of Walden before I got picked up. But I was informed in no uncertain terms by my PO that this was just that: a one-time pass.

Going back to Walden looking like someone returning from a stay at the county morgue was – as you might imagine – a humiliating and humbling experience. But try to imagine my state of mind when three months later, it happened again.

This time I had truly felt as though I had been pouring my very soul into making that program work for me. And I don't think this was just some ego driven self-deception. I'm sure that all the people who had an interest in seeing me make it would agree that I was sincere and focused. There wasn't even so much as a hint of any covetous desire to use drugs again. But then I got angry. Actually, I got very angry.

I had seen men go absolutely ballistic over the TV remote in prison, but this was *me*. I didn't even particularly care for television. Still, here I was yelling, screaming, and threatening to throw clients out of third-story windows. And over what? Which second-rate video we were going to watch, that's what. It was a ridiculous display, at the end of which I went back to my room, packed my bags and made my way back to Polk, Street.

What a cunning thing this was that lived inside of me. How could I ever hope to win against it? My good intentions meant nothing – what I lacked was power.

Obviously this had nothing to do with any video, or even with anger. The *thing* wanted to be fed, and I was powerless to refuse it. Why couldn't I pray now, as I made my way back to Polk, Street and to my own destruction? Why couldn't I just stop, turn around, go back and apologize? I hadn't actually hit anybody. They would have taken me back. I asked myself many such questions as I made my way back to Polk in search of food for the *thing*. But still I pressed on.

Within an hour I had the stuff back in my body and my body back on the floor, engaged in one of the disgusting sex acts that had by now become my standard for human contact. At that time, I'm sure that I must have thought, "So this is why I do it. It's all about having this kind of sex." Now I would say, "So *what*?" So what, to all of these details, man! This *thing* was not playing with me! It wanted me dead!

This was about power. The devil controls the lower nature, and he'd use *anything* to keep me under his power until the end. This was spiritual warfare - God wanted me alive in Christ, while the devil wanted me dead, and separated from Him forever.

What I didn't understand then – and barely understand now – is that I could not lose. This was the power of God that had been pulling and tugging at me for close to two years at this point. There was no equal battle going on here – only God could be victorious. What I didn't realize as I lay on yet another filthy floor with yet another needle in my arm, was that God Almighty was about to bring me out of this thing in such a way that I'd never come back. I was very quickly approaching my point of complete surrender. I was about to know the power of Jesus Christ for myself.

And so I pressed my way on through what was to be my very last relapse into drug addiction. What I remember most about that last hellish run was the hostile and bitter attitude with which I went about handling my business. I hated "them" – all of them, almost as much as I hated myself and despised my weakness. I hated all the lying and cheating, all the victimizing of innocent people and then all of the victimizing of each other. I hated seeing young people out on the street selling their bodies for more of this garbage. I hated knowing what life in the streets and crystal meth was going to do to them.

And I both hated and feared the rats. I hated not knowing which one of these people was going to send me back to prison over a twenty dollar bag of speed.

So I marched on through this last one, viewing the people and the lifestyle I once loved with loath and contempt.

It was an odd circumstance that I had now landed myself in. I couldn't go back to Walden House – my PO had all but assured me that I was going back to prison if I messed up a second time. Besides, the drugs were already running through my veins, so there was no real desire to stop. The only way I had ever been able to come off of drugs was either by getting sick or going to jail, and this time would be no exception. Within five weeks of the time I left Walden, that thing that always happened to me happened again. One of my "good friends" traded my freedom for their own, and I found myself back in San Quentin.

The first few weeks back in prison, I fluctuated between exhausted sleep and waking despair. Even if I didn't drop dead from AIDS, what on earth would the next few years hold for me?

The very idea of ever using drugs again brought bile up into my throat - while at the same time I had absolutely no confidence that I would ever be able to resist this thing that obviously did not want to let me go.

After I was finished licking my wounds, I buried my head back in the New Testament.

"Maybe I'm destined to be the kind of man," I thought, "who can only feel the presence of God when I'm locked in a cage." But I didn't care. I only knew that the last time I was there in prison, I had felt God. This was the only thing that meant anything to me. In the presence of God there was hope – and I so desperately needed this one thing that I was convinced only He could give me. I fully accepted that I was a dope fiend of the hopeless variety and I believed that only God could save me from myself and from the powers that sought to destroy me.

The Bible told me that I should use the name Jesus. It went on to tell me who He was and where He came from. In the pages of the Gospels I found profound answers to the big questions – the biggest being, how do I know God for myself? And Jesus said, "I am the way, the truth, and the life. Follow me." And the next day He'd say, "Seek and ye shall find; knock and the door shall be opened unto you." And on the next day I'd hear, "Come, all you who are heavily laden, and I will give you rest." Every day, the Lord would speak to me through the pages of the Bible, and every day I'd become more and more convinced of who and what Jesus Christ really was.

A few weeks later, I was sent back to the place where I had been paroled from some nine months before. Of course I was somewhat embarrassed by my failure and return, but in truth I didn't really care very much about the people around me. I was on a mission. When Christ said, "Seek and ye shall find," I took that as my marching orders. Church was not just something I did on Sundays – I went every day that the doors were open, and then went back to my cell and one of the many Bible translations I kept open there. After a couple of months I was able to rent someone's radio for eight or ten dollars a month and it was then, while listening to the Christian radio stations, that I was exposed to "the good, the bad, and the ugly."

Of course this would not be my first go-round with irrational bigotry. Only a few short years earlier, these same venomous voices were trying to convince me that my whole race was only slightly more intelligent than monkeys. Now I was to believe that God did not love me or "my kind". Perhaps it was because of my experience as a black man living in a society dominated by white men that I knew not to expect very much in the way of compassion or understanding from the masses, but I took particular offence at the way people attached the name of Jesus Christ to their hatred. If you hated people based on the fact that they were different than you, why not just call it what it was – hate – and then ask God to help you in your own sinful humanness.

Surely anyone who read the four gospel accounts of the life and times of Jesus Christ must know that He had absolutely nothing to say on the subject of homosexuality. Yet to hear some of this ranting and raving on the radio, you would think that being heterosexual was some kind of essential element of being a Christian.

I smelt a whiff of the enemy in all of this. After all, no matter what the supposed purpose of all of this self-righteous finger-pointing and comparing of sins, the end result was -at best- that you'd stop many people who happened to be gay from seeking Christ, therefore giving the devil the victory in their lives. I don't know why that would be good news to anyone calling themselves a Christian.

But I couldn't afford to be distracted by all of the controversy and human opinion that has surrounded Christianity since its inception. I was a desperate and spiritually hungry man. Maybe someday I'd work my way back around to this level of bickering and sharing of opinions, but for now I only sought to know the Lord. The hope had returned, only this time I understood that the hope was not about me – this time my hope was in Jesus Christ.

I made a decision to trust Him with my life and anything that was to occur after that. The Bible calls this faith, and from this point on I'd call Jesus Christ my Lord and Savior.

Because I wanted to leave no stone unturned and because I wanted to be certain that I was doing all that I could to participate in my own recovery, I got involved in two things aside from my spiritual pursuits. For one, I went back to group therapy (I had started this group the previous time that I passed through the prison), and the other thing was that I decided to try to work the twelve steps of Alcoholics Anonymous again. In truth, even with all of my past experience with AA, I had never made it very far with the steps. The first three were of a spiritual nature and at this point in my life, came as easily as breathing in and out. The fourth, however, required action: making "a searching and fearless moral inventory" of myself. It meant dredging up all of the most sordid details of my painful past. This was as far as I had ever made it following that particular program, so now I tackled it with zeal and painstaking honesty. I figured that as long as I was working steps that I had never attained before, I was making progress.

Part of the fourth step was making a list of every person whom I felt I had reason to resent. Since I started at around the age of three, this list kept me busy for several weeks. But when I was finished, an inner voice ever so gently moved me away from the twelve-step program again. It was as if I was being led by something inside of me that was connected to something outside of me. I was learning that I had to trust and lean on that inner voice. It had to be somehow connected to God, because everything it told me was good.

When I tried to share my hope and excitement over the good news of the gospel of Jesus Christ with my therapy group, one of the guys got very excited. He wanted to tell me that the Book of Leviticus said that all homosexuals should be put to death. This was the very same man that only moments earlier had been talking about his desire to set his father on fire. Maybe this brother did have a screw or two loose, but I learned a valuable lesson about hypocrisy that day. Still the group did seem to work for me, and the concept of group therapy was yet another tool that I would use frequently in my efforts to relearn how to live.

Not every day in group was a good time, however, and after returning to the same place in such a relatively short time, I found that people were not so likely to take me seriously. One day it got a little rough, and when I got back to my cell I decided to write about what I was feeling.

It was while writing these two-and-a-half pages to the best of my ability that I got delivered from drug addiction.

Chapter Nine: Delivered

Deliverance – what a sweet sound this word was to my ears. The implication was that by the power of God a person like me could be set free from whatever held them captive. It seems like every time someone used that word in church, I'd be on my feet. In the prison chapel there were ministers and ministries coming in from all over the state of California, but it was when somebody got up at that pulpit talking about how God had delivered them from X, Y and Z that my very soul would cry out, "Hallelujah!"

This was what I wanted most from the Lord. More than anything else in the world, I wanted to be *free*.

Being free is not the same thing as being in remission. Being in remission means; spending every day in fear of relapse. It means raising my hand (as is the custom in twelve step groups) every day of my life to proclaim to a group and to myself that I am an incurable alcoholic and a drug addict, which for me, only reaffirms the curses of the devil over me. As long as I parroted and magnified his power over me, he would continue to use that power to destroy me. I had danced this particular dance with the enemy of my soul enough times by now to know that, at least in my case, he always won. It was time to rebuke the evil one, and give praise and honor to the Holy One who gives life.

So yes, with every fiber of my being I wanted to be delivered from the clutches of this monster that had held me captive for over sixteen years. The Bible said that the Lord would give me the desires of my heart; I don't see how it would be possible for a human being to want anything more.

I know that some people would argue that deliverance doesn't come in an instant, that this whole two-year process was my deliverance. Others might say that deliverance is tied to the level of surrender, or the force with which a person hits bottom. I will concede that this could be a decent argument – for those who like to argue. Fortunately, I don't count myself among those numbers, at least not when it comes to the workings and movements of the living God.

For me, God remains a wondrous and mysterious supernatural source of life and intelligent power. Knowing and accepting that God has delivered me from a lifetime of drug addiction and profound self loathing is one thing; trying to explain how and exactly when He did it is quite something else.

Still, if pushed for an answer, I'd have to say that I received my deliverance from crystal meth on June 25, 2002 at around 2:30 in the afternoon. I can be so certain of the date and approximate time only because I'm holding in my hand the two sheets of paper that I happened to be writing on that afternoon.

The paper starts out by talking about what a bad time I had had in a group therapy session that day. In fact, I titled the first page "How I'm feeling right now." This quickly turned into a reflection of how I had felt on the day of my blowup and subsequent relapse at Walden several months earlier. As I began writing about the events that occurred immediately after pulling the syringe from my arm, my handwriting deteriorated into a child-like scribble. What was left for the record was something like: "HeLLLLp!!!---PANIC---cRyinG with No Praying JESus please help me!! Over and over I'm SO SICK!! I'm SO SICK! OOOOH! GOD JESUS please help SO sick SEX I have Got to sTOp reLax--- Change Subject."

If a guard or trustee happened to pass by my cell at that particular moment, they certainly got quite an eyeful. But if they were there, I was oblivious to their presence. In fact, I seemed to be in some kind of trance, momentarily catapulted back to the impromptu sex orgy which had been thrown together within an hour after I stepped out of the doors of Walden House that very last time.

It had all started as a game.

As I tried to recall exactly when sex had gone from being simply something that felt good to something that in my emotional scribble was best described as sick, I found that I had to go a long way back. Back to the time that I first started using meth.

I remembered a bizarre incident that happened outside of an after-hours club in Hollywood some fifteen years earlier. At the club that I frequented most often it was the fashion to wear some article of black leather on the dance floor. Some guys wore just a little and others wore way too much, but virtually everybody wore something. At the time I thought of black leather as nothing more than erotic dance floor get-up. People wore whips and paddles tied to their belt loops, handcuffs in regulation police holders, chaps (leather pants with the front and back panels missing), and on and on... there was even the occasional hooded man. I knew that there were sadomasochistic implications behind all this costuming, but for me it was simply an issue of fashion and fitting in.

Early one morning when I wandered outside the club, (which was open from Friday night straight though till Sunday afternoon) for cigarettes or coffee or something, I ran into an old acquaintance. When he saw the leather dog collar around my neck, his face turned as white as a ghost. "What are you doing with that thing around your neck, man?" he demanded. "Take it off now before it's too late! It's not a game, man. What you're doing is dangerous and evil!"

What a loser, I remembered thinking. If there was one thing that I hated more than somebody who couldn't handle there drugs, it was some dude trying to bring down my high.

Now it would appear that I had come full circle: If approached by that same man on the day of this writing and subsequent break though, I would have had absolutely no problem understanding exactly what he was trying to say to me.

Yes, it had all started as a game. Then in the bleak times that followed my clubbing years, sex of any kind had not been a major issue. Frankly, I was far too busy chasing the next hit, trying to stay out of the rain, and perhaps keeping a little food in my stomach to worry about such a mundane thing as sex. But after arriving in San Francisco, when I began dealing in earnest and the emphasis was no longer on the basics, things changed dramatically. I went from being a person who rarely had physical contact with anyone to a person whose very existence revolved around his sex life. After a while I had no unfulfilled sexual fantasies – every time I thought up something new, I simply went out and did it.

What I was to discover about pursuing fantasy and sexual make-believe was that there was a definite progression – or regression, depending on how you look at it – when these fantasies were fueled by drugs. What I ended up stuck in for many years was a very dark place.

At this point I think it senseless to dwell on or make much of this drug-induced foolishness. This was only another trick of the enemy. As long as I felt like there was some mysterious, dark state of ecstasy that could only be accessed by the use of crystal meth – you guessed it, I'd always return to it. There was never any state of ecstasy, only a dark place in my human soul. Like everything else about meth, it was only another illusion – an illusion that I pursued almost unto death.

Say or think what you will about deliverance, I only know that after I got this particular revelation, I never returned to drugs.

And so, when I paroled from prison for the very last time, in October of 2002, I left there a free man. Oh yes, I still had two more years to do on parole, but I had never felt so *free* in my life. There was something deep within me that told me that I would never use drugs again.

Walden House remained unfinished business, and when I left Vacaville I went right back to the house that I had abandoned a year earlier. There was still much that I could gain by returning to program, not the least of which was safe and cheap housing. Maybe in most places housing would not be a major concern, but San Francisco was and is one of the most expensive cities to live in the United States. Being that I was on parole, I couldn't legally leave the Bay Area even if I had wanted to. That's not to say that I didn't benefit greatly by the clinical help, support and resources that I received at Walden. That program was figuratively the bridge that I used to cross over from my old life into the real world.

About three months into my commitment to the program, I lost my temper again, only this time those people at Walden (staff and clients) surrounded me and held on to me. This time I finished the program, and for the first time since grade school, I, Timothy Blaine, actually graduated from something. Maybe to some people graduating from a drug program would represent no major accomplishment, but to me it was monumental. And it was only the beginning.

The voice had said "never" when it spoke to me in Vacaville; it said that I would never do drugs again. Now, here in the year 2002, out in the real world, dare I trust Him? Dare I be unafraid of relapse? Was it possible that God, or Jesus, or the Holy Spirit had actually called this unclean thing out of me forever?

There was then – and without a doubt there will always be – much that I don't understand about the spiritual realm or about how God does all that He does. But my testimony is that He does do this particular thing, and He does it in such a way that is superior to any other way that I've ever come across. So yes, I made a decision to change my language on the subject of my former drug addiction. Since God said I'm delivered, I am delivered. I declare it and receive it by faith. In this instance I am not only talking about faith in God and his power to keep me – I'm also talking about faith in the fact that I heard His voice in the first place.

How does one go about explaining an inaudible voice that you hear without the use of your ears? For this answer I had to go back to the Gospels. Jesus said that after He left this world, the Father would send us a helper. This one would be called the Holy Spirit. The question was, could I accept this teaching as reality, and move on by faith?

My answer to The Lord was then, and is now, "yes." By saying "yes" to God, it means saying, "Yes, I receive as fact that there was and is a Jesus Christ who is alive and sitting at the right hand of God. It means receiving as fact that He died on a cross roughly two thousand years ago as a one-time sacrifice for the sin of this world."

It means accepting that the still small voice that I had been referring to for a full two years at this point was in fact real, and it had a name, more than likely this was the voice of God's Holy Spirit, whom the Bible calls our helper. It also means receiving as fact that our merciful God has declared you and me perfect in his sight, not because of all the self-serving foolishness that we call righteousness, but because God is Good and He's given us the ultimate gift. You and I are blessed beyond reason. We can actually have the righteousness of Jesus Christ in the eyes of our God, and all we have to do is receive it.

I invite anyone who might be reading this right now and who is not yet a Christian to cry out "YES!" to God and to receive Jesus Christ as his or her personal Lord and Savior. I did this as a sick and broken man in an isolated and lonely prison cell several years ago. And God heard me. That's how I know that He's able to hear you too, no matter where you might be. God wants every one of us to come to Him, but from what I understand of what is written we've got to accept His sacrifice. It's God's plan and we don't have to completely understand it to know that it must be good.

The devil will do ANYTHING to stop us from receiving this gift from our Creator. The Bible says that we wrestle not against flesh and blood but against spiritual principalities in high places. I challenge you to push past the enemy and all of his many devices right into the presence of The Living God. God has made a way for us to do just that. That way is by Faith in Jesus Christ.

For my brothers and sisters who happen to be homosexual: think it not strange when religious folk whom you've never met and know nothing about you claim to despise you or who and what you are. I don't know why we should expect unbending religion to treat us better than it treated God's Christ; remember it was religion that conspired to murder Him.

Somehow, we as human beings still want to cling to something that we can see and touch. The Bible is not God. Only God is God and He's not dead or lying dormant in the pages of a book. When God brought forth the Christ and His plan for the salvation of this world, the religious leaders would not receive Him because it meant accepting that God had done something new. They would rather kill Him than to accept a new teaching. Religion was then what it is so often now – it will do anything to protect an antiquated belief system. I would encourage you, my brothers and sisters, not to base what you feel about God on anybody's religion.

When it came time for me to choose a church home, it was not nearly as difficult as I thought it might be. Actually it was much more like my church chose me. What I was to discover about a community church was that it was just that: a community having church. Perhaps for the first time in my life, I was able to fully embrace a community of people who looked a lot like me. I never dreamed that I'd find this camaraderie in a Christian church.

Obviously, I am both African American and gay and I have a lifetime membership in both of those communities, but rarely in my experience did the two overlap. However, I believe that I can honestly say that I didn't choose the place where I would worship based purely on these two significant factors. I chose the place where I would worship God based heavily on how they as a church felt about the finished work of Jesus Christ. Everything from this point forward would have to line up with the unbridled worship of Jesus. It was Christ Jesus who brought me out of both a figurative and literal prison – at long last a free man and it was in Him that I would pledge my allegiance for all the rest of my time on Earth.

If the only way that I would ever be free to worship God and his Christ without being ostracized or made to feel unclean and unforgiven was to do so surrounded by people who looked just like me, then that is how it would have to be. I didn't have time to play the mind games of traditional, organized religion – there was and is far too much at stake.

Even though my desire to use drugs never returned, life in the real world was not without its challenges. During the roughly two years that I was in and out of Walden House, I managed to make only one close friend; his name was Enrique.

Enrique and I were about as close as friends could become in such a relatively short time. In the first year after program, he relapsed on crystal meth. Six weeks later, he was dead. This time I had no drugs to numb the pain of watching my friend die. I was forced to just stand there, flat-footed, and deal with life on life's terms.

In my third year I ran into my very best friend from my many years in and out of prison. While Roosevelt's drug of choice was crack cocaine, mine of course had been meth, so we didn't run in the same circles on the streets. But both of our paths kept leading back to the same place. Because we were not under the influence of anything as long as we were locked up, I knew him much better than I knew anyone else in San Francisco. When I ran into him, Roosevelt was still smoking crack and I was over three years clean, so there was no reason for us to be hanging out with each other. But God knew what we didn't know, and a few weeks later, Roosevelt called me from a hospice; he was then within two months of his death. This time I was able to be there for my friend in his darkest hour, and I knew that it was only the mighty hand of God that had let it be so.

There would of course be many other challenges in the years to come, not the least of which has been a seemingly lightning-quick descent into middle age. I had decided as a young man to live life on the edge and to party until I dropped. But now, by the grace of God, the party was most assuredly over – and I hadn't dropped. No matter how I may have felt on the inside, time had most certainly moved on. I found myself trying to build relationships with nieces and nephews that I had never met and were now entering college. There had been of course no preparation for what life would be like on this side of forty, and HIV made forty five feel more like sixty at times.

But God was and is with me around every twist and turn in the road. What God had spoken into my spirit in that desolate prison cell several years ago had proven true. That inaudible voice I was sure I had been hearing for a full two years before that had also proven true, as evidenced by the faith and deliverance I walk in today. I am convinced above all things that *God is good* and that He both intricately knows and loves this thing – me – that only He has created.

The Spirit of the Lord didn't just take off for parts unknown after I got off drugs. After I discovered the power of the living God for myself, I learned to turn to Him for everything.

Sadly, it was in coming to terms with religious persecution that I needed Him most. I simply could not understand the hatred. Even when I went into the Scriptures myself with what I considered an open mind I found that there was much to be debated when they were taken in context, such as their authors, and to whom they were being written. What I am coming to understand even as I write this sentence now is that I am never going to understand hate, but in fact there's nothing to understand. In the earth there is both love and hate, good and evil, they are both opposing entities. God is love – and surely that other thing originates from another place.

Humanity is what it is, but that doesn't change who God is or what He in his goodness has done for this, His greatest creation. In truth the only time I've ever felt like this world was fair, impartial, and unbiased was at the cross. With the blood sacrifice of Jesus Christ, God has done what no man would ever do – he's made us all the same person. We who believe are all one person, the body of the perfect Christ. It's good news and God didn't restrict it to a people group – after all, what thing that walks or crawls on the earth doesn't belong to God? The event at the cross happened a very long time ago, but it wasn't until I received Jesus Christ as my personal Lord and Savior that I ever experienced any significant or lasting life change.

As I look back over the story of my life, I can plainly see a recurring theme. I am a person whose whole life had been ruled by fear. Starting from my very earliest memories, fear has been intricately woven into every chapter of my experience. Fear of my stepfather's violence, fear of my sexuality, fear of being found out, fear of rejection, fear of AIDS, fear of relapse, and on and on. I've spent a lifetime being afraid. It's interesting that when I tried to describe my very first time using crystal methamphetamine in chapter five of this writing, there were only two things that I could recall that it did for me that first day. One, it sobered me up; and two, perhaps for the first time in my life, the *fear* was gone.

I am convinced that illicit mind-altering drugs are a tool of Satan, as evidenced by the havoc and chaos they inevitably bring in their wake. The enemy wants control of our minds. I got HIV/AIDS because I succumbed to the tricks of that thing which seeks to destroy me. When I began trusting in his chemicals for relief and escape, I wasn't even left with enough sense to realize that sticking a needle in my arm – right at the pinnacle of perhaps the worst blood-born epidemic in the history of the world – was demonic madness.

My testimony is that when Jesus Christ took the fear away, unlike Satan, He didn't replace it with havoc and chaos. Nor did I descend into the belly of an earthly hell. That's what the enemy will do for you. But instead, the fruits of the Holy Spirit are love, joy, peace…. For, "God hath not given us the spirit of *fear*; but of power, and of love, and of a sound mind."(2 Timothy 1:7).

As I close, I want to speak directly to those persons who don't yet know the Lord for themselves, and are still held captive by the vices of this world.

I want to encourage you, my brothers and sisters, to try Jesus Christ. You and I and everybody that walks this planet have access to the very same power. It is the power of God, and I'm a living witness that God is no respecter of persons. If he were, I doubt that a pleasure-crazed drug dealer like me would have made the cut.

God is good and this thing that he has done for us all is most *excellent*. Please don't miss it. Give your faith to Jesus Christ.

And prepare to be amazed.

About the Author

Timothy Blaine is a first time author and a graduate of the school of hard knocks. He currently makes his home in San Francisco with his dog Jimmy.

Printed in the United States
66515LVS00001B/61